Holiness Teachings

Compiled From The Editorial Writings Of The Late

Rev. Benjamin T. Roberts, A.M.,
General Superintendent Of The Free Methodist Church,
Editor Of "The Earnest Christian."
Author Of "Fishers of Men," ETC.

By

Benson Howard Roberts, A.M.
Principal of the A.M. Chesbrough Seminary

First Fruits Press
Wilmore,
Kentucky c2017

Holiness teachings.
Compiled from the editorial writings of Benjamin Titus Roberts by Benson Howard Roberts.

First Fruits Press, ©2017
Previously published by Earnest Christian Publishing House, 1893.

ISBN: 9781621717515 (print), 9781621717522 (digital), 9781621717539 (kindle)

Digital version at
http://place.asburyseminary.edu/firstfruitsheritagematerial/144/

First Fruits Press is a digital imprint of the Asbury Theological Seminary, B.L. Fisher Library. Asbury Theological Seminary is the legal owner of the material previously published by the Pentecostal Publishing Co. and reserves the right to release new editions of this material as well as new material produced by Asbury Theological Seminary. Its publications are available for noncommercial and educational uses, such as research, teaching and private study. First Fruits Press has licensed the digital version of this work under the Creative Commons Attribution Noncommercial 3.0 United States License. To view a copy of this license, visit http://creativecommons.org/licenses/by-nc/3.0/us/.

For all other uses, contact:

First Fruits Press
B.L. Fisher Library
Asbury Theological Seminary
204 N. Lexington Ave.
Wilmore, KY 40390
http://place.asburyseminary.edu/firstfruits

Roberts, Benjamin Titus, 1823-1893.
  Holiness teachings / Benjamin T. Roberts; [compiled] by Benson Howard Roberts. Wilmore, Kentucky: First Fruits Press, ©2017.
      vi, 256 pages; 21 cm.
      Includes index.
      Reprint. Previously published: North Chili, N.Y.: Earnest Christian Publishing House, 1893.
      ISBN - 13: 9781621717515 (pbk.)
      1. Holiness. 2. Sanctification. I. Title. II. Roberts, Benson Howard.
BT767.R64 2017   234.8

Cover design by Jon Ramsey

asburyseminary.edu
800.2ASBURY
204 North Lexington Avenue
Wilmore, Kentucky 40390

First Fruits Press
The Academic Open Press of Asbury Theological Seminary
204 N. Lexington Ave., Wilmore, KY 40390
859-858-2236
first.fruits@asburyseminary.edu
asbury.to/firstfruits

HOLINESS TEACHINGS

COMPILED FROM THE
EDITORIAL WRITINGS OF THE LATE

REV. BENJAMIN T. ROBERTS, A. M.,

GENERAL SUPERINTENDENT OF THE FREE METHODIST CHURCH,
EDITOR OF "THE EARNEST CHRISTIAN."
AUTHOR OF "FISHERS OF MEN," ETC.

BY

BENSON HOWARD ROBERTS, A. M.
Principal of the A. M. Chesbrough Seminary.

NORTH CHILI, N. Y.:
"EARNEST CHRISTIAN" PUBLISHING HOUSE.
1893.

COPYRIGHT, 1893, BY B. H. ROBERTS.

CONTENTS.

CHAPTER I.—A SUMMARY. Sanctification and Holiness synonomus, what holiness implies, a sanctified body, distinct from justification, holiness necessary to qualify for heaven, to present happiness, to usefulness, its attainableness, commanded, examples, how attained, confession, faith, presumption. Pages 1-12.

CHAPTER II.—HOLINESS NOT UNDERSTOOD. Difference of opinion as to meaning, not recognized in Job, in Christ, His warning to His disciples, Wesley, Whitefield defamed, professors of holiness condone popular sins, slavery, secretism, persecution of holy men, false standard, not absolute perfection. Pages 13-19.

CHAPTER III.—NATURE OF HOLINESS. Edwards on holiness of God, of man derived, not the result of refinement, or discipline, being not doing, Christ's order reversed, Wesley's " Almost Christian" retrogression. Pages 20-24

CHAPTER IV.—PROPERTIES OF HOLINESS. Negative characteristics, intolerant of false worship, consideration of Scriptures commonly held to teach necessity of sin. Pages 25-33.

CHAPTER V.—ATTRIBUTES OF HOLINESS—DELIVERANCE FROM PRIDE. Roman Catholic teaching, purity without pride, pride in children, denominational pride. Pages 33-39.

CHAPTER VI.—ATTRIBUTES OF HOLINESS—UNSELFISHNESS. Selfishness, self-love, regulated, selfishness sanctioned by pew renting, church fairs, enabled by grace to take a stand against these, holiness and selfishness cannot dwell together. Pages 40-44.

CHAPTER VII.—ATTRIBUTES OF HOLINESS—CONTROL OF APPETITES. Holiness precludes unlawful and inordinate indulgence, saves from depraved appetites, tobacco, opium, spirits, holiness gives deliverance. Pages 45-51.

CHAPTER VIII.—ATTRIBUTES OF HOLINESS—LOVE. Holiness frees from hatred, hostility, prejudice, envy. Pages 52-56.

CHAPTER IX.—ATTRIBUTES OF HOLINESS—HATRED OF SIN. Slavery condoned by spurious holiness, also popular sins, true holiness recognizes, hates, opposes sin in self, others, is aggressive, will ensure persecution, and enable one to stand. Pages 57-64.

CHAPTER X.—ATTRIBUTES OF HOLINESS—HONESTY IN BUSINESS. Justice done in business, no advantage taken because of lack of knowledge or because of position. Pages 65–68.

CHAPTER XI.—ATTRIBUTES OF HOLINESS—IMPARTIALITY. Brotherhood of man recognized, in free seats in churches, in giving respect to character not rank or wealth. Pages 65–72.

CHAPTER XII.—ATTRIBUTES OF HOLINESS—LOVE TO GOD. This is supreme, shown by desires to please Him, to know His will revealed in the Bible, in nature, by supporting only those who preach truth, by obedience to all His commands, by a spirit of devotion, by praises. Pages 72–79.

CHAPTER XIII.—ATTRIBUTES OF HOLINESS—TRUST IN GOD. For grace, in emergencies, for temporal help in trials. Pages 79–84.

CHAPTER XIV.—ATTRIBUTES OF HOLINESS—LOVE TO MAN. Interest in others, especially in brethren in Christ, shown by early Christians, not an indiscriminate love, love to enemies. Pages 85–89.

CHAPTER XV.—JOY. Not of earthly origin, undervalued, scripture instances, and teaching, also of Wesley, Edwards, and hymns, essential. Pages 90–96.

CHAPTER XVI.—EXAMPLES OF HOLINESS. Abel, Enoch, Noah, Job. Pages 97–111.

CHAPTER XVII.—LIMITS OF SANCTIFICATION. Sin in any form incapable of sanctification, money worship, pride, the drama, the attempt, a cause of corruption to the church. Pages 111–116.

CHAPTER XVIII.—A PRESENT EXPERIENCE. Not placed in the future, present deliverance possible. Pages 117–120.

CHAPTER XIX.—HOW OBTAINED. Determination, independence, self-sacrifice, "sanctify yourselves," confession, trust. Pages 121–128.

CHAPTER XX.—HOW RETAINED. Respect to scriptural teachings, things to be done, kept by power and love of God. Pages 129–133.

CHAPTER XXI.—HOW LOST. Yielding to temptation, relationship of him who has lost holiness, doubts, unbelief, experience of Fletcher, can one lose holiness without losing justification, degrees of holiness. Pages 134–142.

CHAPTER XXII.—PROFESSING HOLINESS. Necessity, be definite, unfounded professions, lack in professors, not temperate, conformed to the world in dress, humility, profess holiness if you have it, a false holiness, Methodist Discipline condemns. Pages 143-154.

CHAPTER XXIII.—A POWERLESS PROFESSION. Want of usefulness, seek perfect love, confess your lack. Pages 155-158.

CHAPTER XXIV.—KINDS OF HOLINESS. True holiness, characteristics, aristocratic, fanatical, covetous holiness. Pages 159-163.

CHAPTER XXV.—DEFECTIVE HOLINESS. Ineffective because defective, in spirituality, loyalty to church rather than to God, early church, Luther, Wesley. Pages 163-170.

CHAPTER XXVI.—FALSE HOLINESS. Based on false assumption, and teachings, sanctification a change not only in relation but in nature, teaching of 1 Thes. 23-4. Pages 171-178.

CHAPTER XXVII.—A FIGHTING HOLINESS—SANCTIFICATION IN STREAKS. Holiness not quarrelsome, not compromising, but unyielding to evil, sanctified in streaks. Pages 179-182.

CHAPTER XXVIII.—HOLINESS BEFORE THE LORD. Scripture warning of counterfeits, marks of the genuine. Pages 183-188.

CHAPTER XXIX.—PROMOTING HOLINESS. Reasons for little done, how it may be done, face the truth, point out inconsistencies in professed Christians, knowledge of the doctrine, baptized by the Holy Ghost. Pages 189-195.

CHAPTER XXX.—HOLINESS OPPOSED. In the Church, reasons. Pages 195-290.

CHAPTER XXXI.—JUSTIFICATION AND ENTIRE SANCTIFICATION DISCRIMINATED. Explanation of 1, Cor. 1;2, and chapter following, degrees of sanctification, true works of grace, definiteness, holiness, entire sanctification, perfect love. Pages 201-206.

CHAPTER XXXII.—PERFECTION. Prejudice against the term, New Testament use, meaning, progressive perfection, not perfect by faith, perfection not sanctification, not sought by prayer alone. Apostolic example, perfect service, always necesearily imperfect in some things, perfect love not cross, unkind. Pages 206-216.

CHAPTER XXXIII.—DEAD TO SIN. Lack of this death in professors of holiness shown by fear to speak against popular sin, lack of love, self will, crucifiction to sin, how obtained, results. Pages 217-223.

CHAPTER XXXIV.—ROOTS OF BITTERNESS. Troublesome things in pulpit and church. Pages 224-226.

CHAPTER XXXV.—BE YE HOLY. God's command, importance, features examined. effects on life, possibility of obedience. Pages 227-234.

CHAPTER XXXVI.—ARE YOU HOLY? Importance of the

question, provision made for holiness, the word of God. Pages 235-238.

CHAPTER XXXVII.—THE CARNAL MIND. Consideration of Greek words rendered "mind," the carnal mind set on things earthly, sanctification turns the affections heavenward. Pages 238-243.

CHAPTER XXXVIII.—SEEKING HOLINESS. Omit the "if," put off the old, separation to God, the work of faith, the result, dying daily, feeling not evidence, the refining fire. Pages 244-254.

PREFACE.

In January 1860 was issued at Buffalo, N. Y., the first number of *The Earnest Christian* by my beloved father. In the introductory article he states "*The doctrine of Christian Holiness* as taught by Wesley and Fletcher, being as we conceive plainly enforced in the Word of God and constituting the real strength and power for good of the Church of Christ will occupy a prominent place in our columns." Readers of *The Earnest Christian* will testify that this promise was amply redeemed. For more than a quarter of a century his pen was busy with topics vital to godliness. The subject of Holiness was a constantly recurring theme.

This book is a compilation of the editorials written in the interval of the years 1860-1893. It necessarily must follow that there be some repetition of illustration and phraseology in articles written during such an extended period of time, without the logical connection that attaches to a formal treatise.

Immediately following the death of my father, Feb., 27, 1893, there came a demand for the publication of a collection of his editorial writings. The work has been undertaken amidst the exacting demands of school work, it has been a labor of love, and of personal spiritual good. The reception accorded this venture, will decide as to the publication of other volumes on other topics.

That this book may go forth to bless the world, with a fuller light and knowledge of God's good will to man, is my hope, my prayer. Amen.

BENSON HOWARD ROBERTS,

A. M. Chesbrough Seminary,

North Chili, N. Y.

JUNE 29, 1893.

HOLINESS TEACHINGS.

CHAPTER I.

A SUMMARY.

WE propose to examine this all important subject in the light of the Bible. One plain text of the Scriptures proves more than a thousand human assertions.

The words sanctification and holiness, as used in the Bible, mean the same thing. The same Greek word, ἁγιασμός, is translated in our Bible, sometimes by the word, holiness, and sometimes by the word, sanctification. The same is true of the word translated, sometimes holy, and sometimes saint. The original is one and the same word.

1. Holiness implies, in common with a state of justification, or pardon, *victory over outward sin*. A person that is holy does not commit sin. This is also true of one who lives justified before God. "For sin shall not have dominion over you, for ye are not under the law, but under grace,"

That is, grace has the mastery over you. In the struggle between grace and sin, grace triumphs. "Whosoever is born of God doth not commit sin."—I John 3:9. But, "Sin is the transgression of the law." So that he who imagines that he enjoys the blessing of holiness, and yet does what God in his word forbids, or neglects to do what he commands, *is deceived*. His so-called *faith* is fatal *presumption*.

2. *Holiness is a state.* It does not consist of a repetition of good acts, but is the gracious condition of the soul which prompts to the performance of all good actions. It is the pure fountain from which pure water continually flows. Proof: "Because it is written, Be ye holy; for I am holy."—I Peter 1:16. This does not say, *Do* holy things, but BE HOLY. "To the end he may stablish your hearts unblameable in holiness." —I Thes. 3:13. It is the *heart* that is to be established; then the habits will be right, of course. These texts show that holiness is a state, and not merely good habits, much less simply a relation.

3. Holiness implies *deliverance from all wrong dispositions, tempers and desires;* and from all inclination to indulge those that are right, in an unlawful manner, or to an inordinate degree. There are dispositions of the soul that are wrong in themselves, such as *anger, pride, and covetousness*. From all wrong tempers a holy person is so far delivered that he not only does not yield

to them, but he does not feel them. Other desires become sinful only when indulged in an unlawful manner, or to an inordinate degree. Our Saviour hungered. In this he did not sin, but he would have sinned, if he had yielded to the temptations of Satan to satisfy His hunger in an unlawful manner. Enoch walked with God, and begat sons and daughters. In a holy person all his powers of body and mind are brought into harmony with the will of God.

"And the very God of peace sanctify you wholly; and I pray God your whole spirit and soul and body be preserved blameless unto the coming of our Lord Jesus Christ."—I Thes. 5:23. This prayer teaches:

(1.) That the body is so far sanctified as to be blameless. For it must be so, before it can be preserved in that state. Hence, when the victim of the use of tobacco, or of strong drink, is sanctified, his body undergoes such a change, through the power of the Spirit of God, that he no longer feels the terrible cravings for indulgencies, which were fast hastening him on to destruction.

(2.) The affections, passions, desires, and propensities are so subdued that they are the occasion of good, and not of harm.

(3.) The intellect, the judgment, the will, and the imagination, are made pure and holy in all their exercises. "Having therefore these promises, dearly beloved, let us cleanse ourselves from all filthiness of the flesh and spirit, perfecting holiness in the fear of God."—II Cor. 7:1. Here we see that holiness is opposed to all *filthiness*, either of body or mind. It removes from soul and body everything that defiles. "Therefore, brethren, we are debtors, not to the flesh, to live after the flesh. For if ye live after the flesh, ye shall die: but if ye through the Spirit, do mortify the deeds of the body, ye shall live."—Rom. 8:12, 13. He that does not live after the flesh does not bring forth the works of the flesh. These are: "Adultery, fornication, uncleanness, lasciviousness, idolatry, witchcraft, hatred, variance, emulations, wrath, strife, seditions, heresies, envyings, murders, drunkenness, revellings, and such like: . . . they which do such things shall not inherit the kingdom of God."—Gal. 5:19-21. They who are holy are led by the Spirit, and bring forth the fruit of the Spirit, which is "Love, joy, peace, longsuffering, gentleness, goodness, faith, meekness, temperance."—Gal. 5:22, 23.

4. *Holiness is distinct from justification*, and *subsequent* to it. When one is converted, he is so far made holy that he has victory over sin. But sin remains, though it does not reign.

"And I, brethren, could not speak unto you as unto spiritual but as unto carnal, even as unto babes in Christ."—I Cor. 3:1. These persons were "brethren," "babes in Christ." Therefore they were justified—they were not sinners, or backsliders, yet they were carnal—not yet made holy. A celebrated minister of the Gospel, suddenly attacked by disease, was recommended to drink brandy. He took a small quantity, and being unused to it, its effects were painfully visible. He was drunk, yet not a drunkard. So these believers were carnal—there were divisions among them, as is too often the case, over the respective merits of their favorite preachers—yet they were *not carnally minded*. In the main, their lives were in accordance with the precept of the Gospel.

"And the very God of peace sanctify you wholly."—I Thes. 5:23. This language implies that they were sanctified in part. Paul says that he remembered, without ceasing, their "work of faith and labor of love, and patience of hope in our Lord Jesus Christ." He says they were worthy of imitation by believers in the regions around, "So that ye were ensamples to all that believe in Macedonia and Achaia."—I Thes. 1:7. Therefore they were not deluded, self-deceived, unconverted men and women who had crept into the church for the sake of popularity. Nor were they backslidden from God. Yet they needed to have God do a farther work for them—to sanctify them wholly.

"Therefore, leaving the principles of the doctrine of Christ, let us go on unto perfection."—Heb. 6:1.

These persons were living in the principles of the doctrine of Christ. They were justified believers. Paul exhorts them to go on to a perfection of holiness.

Do not these plain passages abundantly sustain all we have said as to the nature of holiness?

II.—ITS NECESSITY.

1. It is indispensably necessary *to qualify us for heaven*. We cannot get there without it. None ever did, and none ever will. "Follow peace with all men, and holiness, without which no man shall see the Lord."—Heb. 12:14. "To see God," is to be in His presence, to enjoy the bliss He alone can impart. So that, unless he "Follows peace with all men and holiness," no one, no matter what his church or his creed, can stand before the throne of God. "These are they which came out of great tribulation, and have washed their robes and made them white in the blood of the Lamb."—Rev. 7:14. But "white robes" are the emblem of purity. (Rev. 19:8.) "Who shall ascend into the hill of the Lord? or who shall stand in his holy place? He that hath clean hands, and a pure heart; who hath not lifted up his soul unto vanity, nor sworn deceitfully."—Ps. 24:3, 4. God's holy place is heaven. But only those who are pure in heart, and clean in life shall dwell there.

2. Holiness is indispensable to *present happiness*. The unholy person cannot be happy. He

may enjoy pleasure; but pleasure is not happiness. People seek after pleasure because they are unhappy. The pleasures of the world are short-lived and unsatisfactory. But he who is holy has a never-failing spring of enjoyment within. "In whom, though now ye see him not, yet believing, ye rejoice with joy unspeakable, and full of glory."—I Peter 1:8. "The voice of rejoicing and salvation is in the tabernacles of the righteous."—Ps. 118:15.

3. Holiness is essential to *usefulness*. Unholy men may spread Christianity, but they pervert it as they spread it. Their "riches are corrupted," and they corrupt Christianity when employed for its support. Perhaps no man ever devoted so much wealth for the spread of the Gospel as Constantine; and no one ever did so much to corrupt it. An impure channel will foul the purest water. Colored glass imparts its own hue to the light that passes through it. A holy soul alone is qualified to lead others into holiness. "Create in me a clean heart, O God; and renew a right spirit within me. Cast me not away from thy presence and take not thy holy spirit from me. Restore unto me the joy of thy salvation; and uphold me with thy free Spirit. Then will I teach transgressors thy ways; and sinners shall be converted unto thee."—Ps. 51:10-13. One may, without a clean heart, or the joy of salvation, convert people to the church, but it is

to be feared that few of them will be found to be converted to the Lord.

"And they were all filled with the Holy Ghost, and began to speak with other tongues. Then they that gladly received his word were baptized: and the same day there were added unto them about three thousand souls."—Acts 2:4, 41. Holiness is power. He that possesses it can do good. "For the kingdom of God is not in word, but in power."—I Cor. 4:20.

III.—ITS ATTAINABLENESS.

1. *God commands it.* "Sanctify yourselves therefore, and be ye holy: for I am the Lord your God."—Lev. 20:7. "But as he which hath called you is holy, so be ye holy in all manner of conversation."—I Pet. 1:15. God never commands that which is impossible. To affirm that he does is blasphemous. It would make him out a tyrant.

2. *To sanctify the soul or make it holy, is God's work.* If this can be proved, then it follows that holiness is possible. With Him things are easy that are impossible for men. "Then will I sprinkle clean water upon you and ye shall be clean: from all your filthiness, and from all your idols, will I cleanse you. A new heart also will I give you, and a new spirit will I put within you: and I will take away the stony heart out of your flesh. And I will give you a heart of flesh, and I will put my Spirit within

you, and cause you to walk in my statutes, and ye shall keep my judgments and do them."—Ezek. 36:25-27. Here God says He will do the work, and do it thoroughly. (1.) He will cleanse —not from some,—but from ALL idols, and from ALL filthiness. (2.) He will give a new heart and a new spirit. (3.) He will cause us to walk in His statutes and judgments. He will impart the spirit of obedience, and with it the power to obey.

"Sanctify them through thy truth, thy word is truth."—John 17:17. "And the very God of peace sanctify you wholly."—I Thess. 5:23. These passages plainly imply that it is God's work to make believers holy.

3. *Some have attained to holiness.* (1.) Enoch walked with God three hundred and sixty-five years.—Gen. 5:21, 22.

(2.) Noah was a just man and perfect in his generations, and Noah walked with God.—Gen. 6:9.

(3.) Job was perfect and upright, and one that feared God and eschewed evil.—Job 1:1.

(4.) In the New Testament, the disciples of Jesus are called Christians but three times, never Methodists, Baptists, or Presbyterians. Over sixty times they are called Saints, or the holy ones.

IV.—HOW IT MAY BE ATTAINED.

If it is by the power of God that we are sanctified, then why are not all, and especially all professing Christians holy? Because they do not meet the conditions. These are:

1. Giving one's self fully to God. All of time, talent, property, reputation influence, yea life itself, must be handed over to God to be His for ever. "I beseech you therefore, brethren, by the mercies of God, that ye present your bodies a living sacrifice, holy, acceptable unto God, which is your reasonable service."—Rom. 12:1. The body includes all. A living sacrifice is a constant, perpetual one.

"For I am the Lord your God; ye shall therefore sanctify yourselves, and ye shall be holy: for I am holy."—Lev. 11:44. That is, set yourselves apart for God's service, and he will make you holy.

"For whosoever will save his life shall lose it; but whosoever will lose his life for my sake shall save it."—Matt. 16:25.

1. *Confession of all sin actual or inbred.* "If we confess our sins, he is faithful and just to forgive us our sins, and to cleanse us from all unrighteousness."—I John 1:9. If we confess our actual sins he is faithful and just to forgive us. If we confess our inbred sins he is faithful and just to cleanse us from all unrighteousness.

3. *Faith in Christ as our sanctifier.* "God put no difference between us and them, purifying their hearts by faith."—Acts 15:9. "That they may receive forgiveness of sins, and inheritance among them which are sanctified by faith that is in me."—Acts 26:18.

But beware that your so-called faith is not presumption. Otherwise you may become a self-conceited Pharisee, instead of a humble, meek, holy follower of Jesus. "How can ye believe which receive honor one of another, and seek not the honor that cometh from God only."— John 5:44.

In both these passages faith is spoken of as the medium through which sanctification is received.

Reader, what do you think of these passages of Scripture that we have brought before you? Do they not show you the necessity and the attainability of holiness? Do you live in this state of grace? If so, thank God, and press forward. If not, make no delay to obtain it. You have too much at stake to live without it a single day. Resolve that you will be holy. Ask God to search you! If, in the light of the Spirit, you see, as is often the case, that you are not justified, have the courage and honesty to confess your condition. If in a backslidden state you seek for holiness, you will, in all probability, take up with something short of reality. Be thorough! Confess as fully as the word and the Spirit of God direct. Give yourself up without the least reserve to obey the Lord in everything. Look to Jesus as your present Saviour from all sin. Plead His promises. Rely upon His grace to save you to the uttermost. Thus you shall soon feel the sanctifying power of the Spirit of

God all through soul and body. You will then, in your daily life, have your fruit unto holiness; and the witness of the Spirit will be given, to assure you of your present gracious state, and to give you a pledge of untold glories to be enjoyed in the world to come.

"Now we have received, not the Spirit of the world, but the Spirit which is of God; that we might know the things that are freely given to us of God."—I Cor. 2:12.

CHAPTER II.

HOLINESS NOT UNDERSTOOD.

THE Bible has much to say about holiness. It is an attribute of God. (Ps. 60:6; Rev. 4:8, *et al*). We are commanded to follow it. (Heb. 12:14). To worship God in the beauty of holiness. (Ps. 29:2). Without it no man shall see the Lord. (Heb. 12:14). It is the one thing needful. There are many things which are convenient and useful; but this alone is indispensable to our welfare both in this world and in the world to come.

It is important, then, that we have correct ideas of its nature. If we would hit a mark we must know where to aim. If we would attain an excellence we must know what it is. He who would search for diamonds, must know diamonds when he finds them.

Upon first view, it may seem that men are pretty well agreed as to what constitutes holiness. But, on reflection this will be seen to be a mistake. Upon this point there is a wide diversity of opinion. Such is the imperfection of language and such the constitution of particular minds that the same words often fail to express the same idea to different persons, even when they are equally candid. But take holiness in its most tangible form—take it as exemplified in the lives of holy persons, and it is not generally acknowledged to be holiness. It is usually called by almost any other name than holiness. In God's sight, Job was a holy person. He says, "Hast thou considered my servant Job, that there is none like him in the earth, a perfect and an upright man, one that feareth God and escheweth evil?"—Job 1:8. But even his friends labored to convince him that he was a wicked man. Eliphaz says to him, "They that plough iniquity and sow wickedness, reap the same."—Job 4:8. Bildad takes up the accusation and reminds him that "The hypocrite's hope shall perish."—Job 8:13. Zophar asks him, "Should thy lies make men hold their peace?"—Job 11:3. And even Elihu exclaims, "What man is like Job, who drinks up scorning like water? Which goeth in company with the workers of iniquity, and walketh with wicked men."—Job 34:7, 8. This was the opinion which his friends had of him, as expressed to his face. Of course the judgment of his enemies was much more unfavorable.

Our Saviour exemplified holiness in its most perfect form. In His life, His conversation, His spirit, and in all His actions He was holiness personified. He gave the most unmistakable proofs of disinterested love to all mankind. Yet the popular verdict concerning Him was, "Behold a man gluttonous, and a wine-bibber, a friend of publicans and sinners."—Matt. 11:19.

Christ told his disciples that they must not expect to be appreciated any better than He was. "If they have called the Master of the house Beelzebub, how much more shall they call them of his household?"—Matt. 10:25. From that day down to the present, holiness in the disciples of Christ has been recognized by but few, even of those who call themselves Christians. John Wesley stated clearly, defended ably, and exemplified in his life the doctrine of holiness.— Whitefield for burning zeal, and simple devotion to the cause of Christ, has not had a superior since the days of St. Paul; yet the Rev. Sidney Smith, a clergyman of the same church as that to which Wesley and Whitefield belonged, and a writer of great celebrity, but expressed the estimate in which they were held by their fellow clergymen, when he said: "They were men of considerable talent; they observed the common decorums of life; they did not run naked into the streets or pretend to the prophetical character;—and therefore they were not committed to Newgate. They preached with great energy to weak people, who first stared, then listened— then believed—then felt the inward feeling of grace, and became as foolish as their teachers could possibly wish them to be;—in short, folly ran its ancient course;—and human nature evinced itself to be what it always has been, under similar circumstances. The great and permanent cause, therefore, of Methodism, is the cause which has given birth to fanaticism in all ages—*the facility of mingling human errors with the fundamental truths of religion.*"

In our day we see that which we deem essential to holiness purposely omitted in instructions upon this subject. Popular sins are, to say the least, silently tolerated. During the war of the rebellion, in a popular meeting for the promotion of holiness, in the city of New York, Rev. D. F. Newton thanked the Lord for President Lincoln's Emancipation Proclamation. He was at once called to order for introducing a topic calculated to disturb the harmony of the meeting. There are many works on the subject of holiness, written in the days of slave-holding to circulate among slave-holders, and not a word to be found in them condemning the practice. The same spirit which led to silence respecting the sin of slave-holding in the days when all the popular churches welcomed slave-holders to their communion, to-day utterly ignores the existence of sins which God's word plainly condemns, but which the leading churches openly tolerate. That which encourages what God forbids is not holiness. The name of a thing does not give it its nature.

There is a powerful secret society, spreading itself throughout the country, composed largely of unbelievers, to which, however, many ministers and church-members belong. This society is thoroughly anti-christian in its character. To pray in the lodge in the name of Christ is declared by the highest Masonic authority, to be a violation of the fundamental principles of Masonry. The members bind themselves by the most horrid oaths to submit to be murdered, and to conceal, and even commit murder under certain circumstances. Of these facts any intelligent person can easily satisfy himself beyond the shadow of a doubt. Yet in many meetings held for the promotion of holiness, to point out these hindrances to the work of holiness would be considered impertinent and fanatical.

Again the persecution to which the saints of God have always been subjected shows that holiness is not recognized when seen. The word declares, "Yea, and all that will live godly in Christ Jesus shall suffer persecution."—II Tim. 3:12. This persecution varies in its form with the prevailing spirit of the age. But whatever shape it assumes, persecution never assigns as its reason, the godliness of its victims. Their obstinancy, or contumacy, or disloyalty, or heresy is assigned as the cause of their sufferings.

Christ was put to death as an impostor. Luther was excommunicated as a heretic, and Wesley and Whitefield were hunted as fanatics. Their persecutors were the professed children of God, and they believed it to be a zeal for holiness which instigated their opposition to those who furnished bright examples of holiness in their lives.

On the other hand, there are those who make holiness comprise attributes which are entirely beyond the reach of a human being in our present condition. They give a meaning to the term which the Scriptures do not warrant. According to their standard, a holy person cannot make a mistake in judgment, either through ignorance or misapprehension. He must not only do right, *as he understands it*, but do right as they understand it, under all circumstances. They measure others by their own infallibility. They make no allowance for lack of judgment or for imperfect training. He who professes holiness, must be, according to their views, beyond the reach of unfriendly criticism. In addition to all this, he must never fall. Should he ever afterward manifest any disposition contrary to his profession, it is then assumed that all along he was either deceived or hypocritical. If he lost holiness, the conclusion is not only that he never had holiness, but that no one ever did or ever will! In short, holiness is pronounced unattainable because some who appeared once to have attained it did not persevere to the end.

Thus a false standard of holiness is raised, and then holiness is declared to be an impossibility, because no one is found to come up to this imaginary standard. We are told to aim our arrow at the sun, and then are ridiculed because we fall short of the mark. The moral perfections of God are presented as our standard, and then we are gravely told that we cannot attain it.

CHAPTER III.

NATURE OF HOLINESS.

GOD is a Being of infinite power. He is dependent upon none. All power is derived from Him.

He is also a Being of infinite holiness. This includes all moral perfections. Says Tillotson, "In him there can be no malice, or envy, or hatred, or revenge, or pride, or cruelty, or tyranny, or injustice, or falsehood, or unfaithfulness; and if there be any thing besides which implies sin, and vice, and moral imperfection, *holiness* signifies that the divine nature is at an infinite distance from it."

"The holiness of God," says Edwards, "is the same with the moral excellence of the divine nature, or his purity and beauty as a moral agent, comprehending all his moral perfections, his righteousness, faithfulness, and goodness." His superiority to all false gods, or imaginary deities is found in His moral perfections. "Who is like unto thee, O Lord, among the gods? who is like thee, glorious in holiness, fearful in praises, doing wonders?"—Ex. 15:11. "There is none holy as the Lord."—I Sam. 2:2. "The Lord is righteous in all his ways, and holy in all his works."—Ps. 145:17. "Holy, holy, holy is the Lord of hosts: the whole earth is full of his glory."—Isa. 6:3. This is the nature of the God we worship.

Holiness in man is derived. It is not original, nor innate. It is the image of God's holiness. It resembles His holiness, though it falls infinitely short of it. A tumbler of water taken from the ocean, possesses the same chemical properties as that which remains, though it has not the sublimity, or grandeur, or power of the ocean; so a holy man possesses in a limited degree, the hatred of sin, the sincerity, the veracity, the justice, the love, the goodness, and all the other virtues which constitute in all their fulness the the holiness of God. "Put on the new man which after God is created in righteousness and true holiness.—Eph. 4:24. "What then," says John Wesley, "is that holiness, which is the only qualification for glory? In Christ Jesus," (that is according to the Christian Institution, whatever be the case of the heathen world,) "neither circumcision availeth any thing, nor uncircumcision." It first, through the energy of God, worketh love to God and all mankind; and by this love, every holy and heavenly temper. In particular lowliness, meekness, gentleness, temperance, and long-suffering. It is neither circumcision—the attending on all the Christian ordinances, nor uncircumcision the fulfilling of all heathen morality,—but the keeping the commandments of God; particularly these—'Thou shalt love the Lord thy God with all thy heart, and thy neighbor as thyself;' in a word, holiness is having the mind that was in Christ, and walking as Christ walked."

No matter how much refinement or self-government a man may acquire by discipline—this self-control is not true holiness. Some of the old heathen philosophers lived according to the most rigid rules of morality.

Here is found one fault of much that is taught for holiness in these days. It strives to make men *do better*, without telling them how to *be better*. It lays great stress upon their doing holy things, without insisting upon their being holy. The practical part of Christianity is required of men, without their being taught that they must have its inward experience. The order that Christ established is reversed. The effort is perseveringly put forth to make an evil tree bring forth good fruit. The person whom Wesley describes as an "almost Christian" would, according to the modern theology, be readily accepted as in the enjoyment of holiness. Wesley himself, before he was, according to his own statement, converted to God, might sit as the model for the modern saint. He gave largely.

He was strict in his devotional exercises, and denied himself very rigidly, that he might have to give to the poor. Said a popular Methodist preacher from the pulpit in our hearing: "I thank God the time has come when men's piety is estimated, not by what they profess, but by what they give." In the middle ages warriors, whose hands were red with blood, who had plundered cities by the score, and laid whole countries waste, endeavored to atone for their crimes, by building magnificent cathedrals; and these were accepted by the priesthood as acts and evidences of piety. We are going back to the theology of the tenth century. In the largest denomination of the land, their chief Theological Seminary for the instruction of the future preachers of the church, was built and endowed by one who is notorious as a stock gambler, and whose business transactions are condemned by even the lax, Wall Street morality. In the next largest denomination, the most popular female college was, in like manner, built and endowed by one of the heaviest brewers of the country. The influence of these illustrious examples, is felt in almost every country church. Property controls the pew, and property controls the pulpit. Mammon is the chief minister in Christ's kingdom. The affairs of the church are conducted upon the same business principles as those which control other successful corporations. Experimental piety is branded as fanaticism, which in the poor is not to be endured, and in the rich is only tolerated as a necessary evil.

All this comes from the efforts to build a Christian character with self as the foundation. The seeming success is but a splendid failure. The glittering structure will not stand the first flash of the fires of eternity.

A holy nature comes from God.—Wesley expresses the true sentiment when he sings:

>"I want thy life, thy purity,
> Thy righteousness brought in."

It must be *brought in* to the heart by power divine; it is not there by nature. "The kingdom of heaven is like unto leaven hid in the meal."

CHAPTER IV.

PROPERTIES OF HOLINESS.

GOLD has the same properties in all countries, by whatever name it may be called. The nature of love and of hatred never changes with the lapse of time. Holiness may present different manifestations in different circumstances, but its qualities are as unchanging as its Author. The views of men may vary, but *it* never varies. Examine it in detail or view it as a whole, its qualities never change.

The indistinct notions which many entertain of holiness, are owing to the fact, that they have never seriously considered what it is which constitutes holiness. They are like one who knows nothing of gold but its color, and is therefore ready to call every thing gold which looks like it. He who has any skill in the metals, is not so imposed upon. If he finds one of the required qualities, he searches for another, and not until he finds that a metal possesses *all* the properties that it should, does he pronounce it gold. So if you have holiness, you have all those moral qualities, which taken together, form that grand total of Christian graces, which the word of God denominates holiness. Let us look at some of these qualities.

We will first notice some of the things from which holiness implies deliverance. This is the more necessary, because the self-indulgent spirit which wealth and luxury always beget, lays stress upon a few of the positive properties of holiness, without insisting upon laying aside every thing which is inconsistent with it. But the Bible has quite as much to say about the negative, as about the positive side of holiness. The first commandment reads, "Thou shalt have no other gods before me."—Ex. 20:3. It was not enough to worship the true god—this, Solomon did, even in his backslidden state; but no false god must be worshipped. Of the ten commandments, *nine* contain negative provisions. They tell us what we shall *not* do. Nine prohibitions in the Ten Commandments, and but two positive precepts! From this we might infer that God sees that there is much greater difficulty in keeping us from doing wrong, than there is in leading us, in other respects, to do right. "Herod heard John gladly and did many things," but he would not put away the woman with whom he was unlawfully living.

Cease to do evil; learn to do well (Isa. 1:16), is God's order. To require this, makes trouble. The Romans never scrupled to add another god to their Pantheon. They would readily have admitted Christ to that honor. But when the uncompromising Apostles demanded that their false gods should first be dethroned, Christ was rejected, and his disciples thrown to the wild beasts and to the flames. It was not the purity, so much as the intolerance of Christianity, that stirred up the fierce opposition which it encountered. The martyrs would have avoided their fate, if in addition to worshipping Christ they would have consented to worship Jupiter and Minerva. But they not only maintained that Christianity was true, but that it was *exclusively* true. They not only preached that, "He that believeth and is baptized shall be saved;" but that "he that believeth not shall be damned." They were bold to declare, "Neither is there salvation in any other." No terrors could induce them to join in the cry, "Great is Diana of the Ephesians," or swear by the image of Cæsar. It was this opposition to all that was false, that brought them into trouble wherever they went.

In general, then, holiness implies deliverance from sin. It is the opposite of sin, as light is of darkness.

The Bible teaches us the possibility of having every wrong propensity of the soul destroyed. We are aware that some passages look, at the first view, as though the continuance of sin in the soul was unavoidable. Let us give the more prominent of these a careful and candid examination. The first to which we call attention is found in I Kings 8:46.—"If they sin against thee, (for there is no man that sinneth not.)" In the original Hebrew, the word that is translated "sinneth," is in the future tense. "This tense," says Stuart, in his Hebrew Grammar, page 207, "designates all those shades of meaning which we express in English by the auxiliaries may, can, must, might, could, should, would," etc. Thus "We may eat of the fruit of the trees of the garden."—Gen. 3:2. The term "may eat," is, in the original, in the future tense. So, also, "That they may fear thee."—I Kings 8:40. The phrase, "may fear," is in the future tense in the Hebrew. The same is true of the phrase, "may know," in the forty-third verse, "That all the people of the earth may know thy name." Hence, a literal translation of the forty-sixth verse would read: "If they sin against thee, (for there is no man that may not sin.)" This teaches, not that every man does actually and necessarily sin, but that *every one is liable* to sin. It is *possible* that he may, but not *necessary* that he should sin. So, also, the supposition, "if they sin," implies that they might sin, or they might not. It expresses a contingency that could not exist if sin were unavoidable. That they might not sin, is clearly implied in the declaration that if they did, God would be angry with them, and deliver the

PROPERTIES OF HOLINESS.

into the hands of their enemies, so that they should be carried into captivity. But as this was not necessary, it follows that it was not necessary that they should sin.

Most of the above remarks will apply to the passage found in Eccl. 7:20,—"For there is not a just man upon earth that doeth good and sinneth not." The word, "sinneth," is, in the original, in the future tense, and should also be rendered, "may sin." This passage teaches the doctrine that runs all through the Bible, that we are never secure from the danger of falling. In our best estate, when grace has done the most for us, we have great need to "watch that we enter not into temptation," to "keep our bodies under, and bring them into subjection," lest we should "become castaways."

"Who can say, I have made my heart clean, I am pure from my sin."—Prov. 20:9. This passage is intended to reprove the boasting of a self-righteous, conceited Pharisee, who not only claims a goodness he does not possess, but ascribes his fancied purity to himself. If we offer up, in fervent desire, and a faith that will not be denied, the prayer of David: "Create in me a clean heart, O God," who shall say this prayer will not be answered? God alone is able to purify the soul. It is only by coming to Him in importunate supplication that we can obey the Apostle's direction, "Cleanse your hands, ye sinners, and purify your hearts, ye double-minded."—James 4:8. In this way alone can God's command be met. "O Jerusalem, wash thine heart from wickedness that thou mayest be saved."—Jer. 4:14.

"If I justify myself, my own mouth shall condemn me; if I say I am perfect, it shall also prove me perverse."—Job 9:20. In this chapter Job treats of the majesty and holiness of God. In the 15th verse he says: "Whom though I were righteous, yet would I not answer, but I would make supplication to my Judge." Before the purity of God he counted his righteousness as nothing, however he might lift up his head in the presence of his fellow man. Thus, in the verse above, we understand Job to say: "If I justify myself (before God); mine own mouth," in the prayers that I make for the mercy of the Lord, "shall condemn me." He did justify himself most triumphantly before man, and repelled the accusations which his friends, unable to reconcile his afflictions with the supposition of his innocence, had brought against him. If I say, "I am perfect" in God's sight, of myself, "it shall also prove me perverse." His perfect humility, here manifested, justifies the testimony that the Lord, who cannot be deceived, gives in his favor. "Hast thou considered my servant Job, that there is none like him in the earth, a perfect and an upright man, one

PROPERTIES OF HOLINESS. 31

that feareth God, and escheweth evil."—Job 1:8.

"Who can bring a clean thing out of an unclean? Not one."—Job 14:4. This text refers to the natural depravity that belongs to every one that is born into the world—to what is commonly termed original sin. It teaches that all are by nature depraved, not that this depravity cannot be removed by grace.

The Septuagint—the Greek version of the Old Testament, from which our Saviour and the Apostles generally quoted, thus renders it: "For who is pure from corruption? Not one, although his life upon earth be one day."

"Woe is me! for I am undone; because I am a man of unclean lips."—Isa. 6:5. This is true of all while in their natural, unsanctified condition, yet let us read on and we shall see that the SPIRIT OF GOD, represented by "a live coal" "from off the altar" touched his lips, "so that his iniquity was taken away," and his "sin was purged."

"All our righteousnesses are as filthy rags."—Isa. 64:6. The Jews were exceedingly corrupted in the days of Isaiah. The prophet being humbled and alarmed at the general wickedness of his people, confesses it in the first person, as ministers generally do on such occasions. It is the hypocritical professions of the Jews—a strict observance of the forms and ceremonies of religion while living in sin—that the prophet compares to filthy rags.

"I am carnal, sold under sin."—Rom. 7:14. In this connection, the Apostle speaks of his inward experience: 1. As an unawakened Jew: "I was alive without the law once." 2. As a converted sinner: "But when the commandment came" to my comprehension, "sin revived, and I died;" my hopes perished. 3. As a believer in Christ: "For the law of the Spirit of life in Christ Jesus hath made me free from the law of sin and death." Now, "being made free from sin," and become truly the "servant of God," he had his "fruit unto holiness, and the end everlasting life." That the Apostle, in the above passage, refers to himself prior to his conversion, is the opinion of President Edwards, a Congregationalist divine, who for learning and piety, and philosophical acumen, never had a superior in this country; who says: "The Apostle Paul, speaking of what he was *naturally*, says, 'I am carnal, sold under sin.'"

"If we say that we have no sin, we deceive ourselves, and the truth is not in us."—I John 1:8. That this refers to man in his *natural* condition, is evident. The Apostle is speaking about the power of Jesus' blood *to cleanse us from all sin.* It is those who, falsely and dangerously trusting to their own morality and their naturally amiable dispositions, say that they do not need to be "cleansed from sin," to whom the Apostle applies the above verse. But, being convinced that we are sinners, both by nature and by practice, he assures us that, "if we confess our sins, he is faithful and just to forgive us our sins, and to CLEANSE US FROM ALL UNRIGHTEOUSNESS."—I John 1:9.

These we believe are the strongest passages ever brought forward to prove the necessary continuance of sin. Look at them candidly and you will be satisfied that we have given their true meaning. Let us ask, beloved reader, are you at the present time saved from sin? You may have been once. That cannot help you now. It only makes your condition still more deplorable, if you are still under the dominion of sin. Seek deliverance at once. Give no quarters. Let every sin die. That is a false holiness which does not deliver from all sin. Salvation from sin can alone secure salvation in Heaven.

CHAPTER V.

ATTRIBUTES OF HOLINESS.—DELIVERANCE FROM PRIDE.

THE heart is the seat of sin. Actions derive their moral character from the disposition with which they are performed. To give a sum of money may be an act of benevolence, or it may be bribery,—it may spring from love to Christ, or from love of the praise of men. "For from within, out of the heart of men, proceed evil thoughts, adulteries, fornications, murders, thefts, covetousness, wickedness, deceit, lasciviousness, an evil eye, blasphemy, pride, foolishness. All these evil things come from within, and defile the man."—Mark 7: 21-24.

A justified soul does not yield to sin. "Whosoever is born of God, doth not commit sin."—I John 3:9. A soul sanctified to God wholly does not have sin. "But if we walk in the light, as he is in the light, we have fellowship one with another, and the blood of Jesus Christ his Son cleanseth us from all sin."—I John 1:7. True holiness will save one from sins that are popular, just as readily as from those that are disgraceful.

It is the work of the Spirit. With God, the standard of right does not vary. Selfish considerations lead men to tolerate, sometimes one sin, and sometimes another. A few years ago, many of the advocates of holiness had nothing to say against the sin of slave-holding. The Church gained by it in numbers and resources. Now, many take no decided stand against pride and worldly conformity. They have not a word to utter in condemnation of conspiracies of the strong against the weak. But those who really aim at being right with God, turn from every thing which He has forbidden, even though it is encouraged by the Church.

Holiness implies deliverance from pride. A holy person cannot feel proud. A holy Church cannot indulge in pride. Pride cannot dwell in a holy soul. "Him that hath an high look and a proud heart will not I suffer."—Ps. 101:5. "Be clothed with humility; for God resisteth the proud and giveth grace to the humble."—I Peter 5:5.

In this particular, the Roman Catholics are a reproof to the Protestants. To all who are loyal to the Church, the Catholics give the largest latitude of word and action—of business and pleasure. To keep within the bonds of decency and morality is all that is required of the ordinary members of her communion. You will find among them, ladies as gaily dressed as any that the times can furnish. But they do not profess holiness. Their priests may err in many things, but they do not encourage their people to think that they can become saints, while indulging in pride to the fullest extent that their means will allow. They are taught that if they would become holy, pride must be renounced, and all appearance of pride must be laid aside. But in Protestant churches, you will find persons advocating holiness, whose appearance unmistakably declares that pride reigns within. Their costly apparel, their ornaments of gold, their affected tones, their whole bearing, proclaim that there has been no real renunciation of the vain pomp and glory of the world. This is all wrong, and altogether wrong.

It may be urged that such a course recommends holiness; that it leads the rich and the refined to embrace it. But this is a mistake. It may lead them to embrace a delusion,—to believe that they are sanctified, when they are not even scripturally awakened. That, which is thus recommended, is not holiness. It may have some of its properties, but the essentials are wanting. To make people believe that they can so put on Christ's righteousness as to set off their own purple and fine linen to better advantage, is to make them believe a ruinous lie. Contraries cannot dwell together. Pride and humility can not reign at once in the same heart. Then do

DELIVERANCE FROM PRIDE.

not deceive, even for so good an object as the promotion of holiness. The Saviour has commanded us to count the cost. Until men can see that holiness is more to be desired than all which they are required to give up, they will never obtain it.

"But," many urge, "we should have pride enough to be decent." There is no pride in Heaven. But there is purity. So we may have inward and outward purity, without pride. Pride is a result of the fall. It had no place in Eden. It should have none in all our hearts. Seek then for that holiness which roots it out entirely.

You may make a consecration to the Lord ever so full in other respects, but if it does not include the giving up of your pride in all its forms, you will not get an experience which will enable you to do the will of God. And just in proportion as you give up pride and long for deliverance from it, just in that proportion will God take it from your heart. It is a dangerous foe—give it no quarter. It is a subtle foe, lying in ambush for your overthrow—give it no place for concealment.

Holiness implies deliverance from pride, as manifested in the provision which we make for our children. Pride is one of the sad effects of the fall. It will manifest itself in some form or other in our children, until they are brought completely under the influence of divine grace. But parents, who are wholly sanctified to God, will not give it any encouragement. It needs no fostering. Do what you can to prevent it; from the atmosphere around, it will drink in enough nourishment to grow with alarming rapidity. Cut it back all you may, and with each coming season it will put forth new vigor, and manifest the utmost tenacity of life. As long as you find in yourself a disposition to encourage display in your children,—to fit them up to shine with worldly splendor, you may rest assured that the work of holiness in yourself is not yet complete. You are not fully delivered from pride.

Holiness implies deliverance from denominational pride. There are many who dress plain, and who furnish their houses plain, who will nevertheless give their thousands towards the construction of a church, when every accommodation could be secured for one-third the amount paid for its construction. Two-thirds of all that is paid for our fine houses of worship, is expended for display, and answers no purpose except to gratify pride. One denomination builds a fine church. The next one that builds puts forth every possible exertion to surpass it in magnificence. To raise money, festivals and lotteries are resorted to, and in some cases, downright dishonesty is practised. The fine church must be filled with finely dressed people, and so pride and extravagance are encouraged and the poor virtually excluded from the house of worship. If the true Gospel course were taken by all who call themselves by the Christian name,—if the money expended to gratify pride were judiciously employed in spreading the truth as it is in Jesus, the time would soon come when it could be said in all parts of the world, "The poor have the Gospel preached to them."—Matt. 11:5.

CHAPTER VI.

ATTRIBUTES OF HOLINESS.—UNSELFISHNESS.

WHEN the angel announced the coming of the Saviour, he said, "Thou shalt call his name JESUS: for he shall save his people from their sins."—Matt. 1:21. This, then, is the grand peculiarity of the disciples of Christ, they are a *saved* people. By nature they are no better than others. Grace makes them to differ. And the grand distinction is found in what they are saved from. There are dispositions and appetites which in themselves are sinful. They answer no good purpose. They were not a part of man's nature at the beginning. They result from the fall. No one is sanctified wholly till he is saved from these depraved dispositions and appetites.

Holiness implies deliverance from selfishness. A selfish person cannot, at the same time, be a holy person. Selfishness is that disposition which prompts us to seek our own interests or our own gratification without due regard to the rights or happiness of others. The second great commandment is, "Thou shalt love thy neighbor as thyself."—Matt. 19:19. This certainly supposes that we are, within proper limits, to love ourselves. The Scriptures not only allow, but command us, to have a due regard for our own happiness. Every promise of the Bible is based upon the principle that it is right for us, within proper limitations, to pursue our own welfare. Abraham, in going out from his father's house, "Looked for a city which hath foundations, whose builder and maker is God."—Heb. 11:10. Moses, in giving up the treasures and honors of Egypt, "had respect to the recompense of reward."—Heb. 11:26.

But this principle, so proper in itself, must be carefully regulated, and kept within the bounds which God has prescribed, or it becomes sinful and pernicious. Self-love takes into account the whole of our existence for time and for eternity. Selfishness looks at present interest, and present gratification. Self-love has due respect for the happiness of others; selfishness inclines us to seek our own gratification without regard to the duties which we owe, either to God or to our neighbor. Self-love is a principle which God gave man for his own preservation: selfishness is the sinful substitute which man at the fall adopted. The one is the alcohol which maddens: the other is the corn that gives strength, and the delicious grape that gives health to man.

There is scarcely a crime which man commits,

or a sin of which he is guilty, which does not originate in selfishness. It is the bitter fountain in which every corrupt stream has its source. It is the evil tree which bears every manner of pernicious fruit. It is a vice that is never satisfied; it grows by what it feeds upon. The more it is gratified, the more inordinate are its cravings. It becomes most intense when there is least apology for its existence. It has the utmost tenacity of life, and never dies a natural death. It can be slain, only by the Sword of the Spirit —it can be destroyed only by the fire of the Holy Ghost. It can wear out the strongest constitution, but it is never worn out itself. It exists under a thousand different forms, and in every state of society. The most refined, and the most highly educated, are as much under its influence as the most ignorant and uncultivated.

Popular churches sanction and foster this selfish spirit, in selling, or renting the seats in their houses of worship. The rich man, if saved from selfishness, would not want, on account of his riches, better accommodations in the house of God, than his poorer brother. The rich and the poor would meet together as brethren, feeling that the Lord is the Maker of us all.

Every effort to raise money for religious or benevolent purposes by means of fairs, festivals, or similar contrivances, is an appeal to selfishness. Thus the sanction of the Church is given

UNSELFISHNESS.

to a corrupt principle which underlies all wickedness and saps the very foundation of the Christian character. It fosters that for the extirpation of which it should put forth its mightiest energies.

Years ago, when we were first brought into the experience of the blessing of holiness, and began to realize something of its importance, we saw clearly that the enjoyment of this grace could never become general in a church, so long as pews were rented, and fairs held for the benefit of the finances of the church. We took our stand firmly against all these appeals to selfishness, as standing in the way of the great work of the Church of Christ—the spreading of Scriptural holiness throughout the land.

Holiness and Selfishness cannot dwell together. When the Spirit was poured out, upon the opening of the Christian dispensation, the selfish spirit was utterly rooted out, "And all that believed had all things common; and sold their possessions and goods, and parted them to all men, as every man had need."—Acts 2:44, 45. Whether this is, or is not, to be regarded as a model for Christians, in all ages, to follow, it is certainly a specimen of the spirit which Christian holiness is to produce. It is an extirpation of the selfish principle.

To this end are such precepts and declarations as these. "Let each esteem other better than themselves. Look not every man on his own things, but every man also on the things of others."—Phil. 2:3, 4.

"For none of us liveth to himself, and no man dieth to himself."—Rom. 14:7.

"But to do good and to communicate, forget not; for with such sacrifices God is well pleased."—Heb. 13:16.

"Bear ye one another's burdens, and so fulfil the law of Christ."—Gal. 6:2.

"Set your affection on things above, not on things on the earth."—Col. 3:2.

CHAPTER VII.

ATTRIBUTES OF HOLINESS.—CONTROL OF APPETITES.

TRUE holiness has its influence on every part of our nature. It affects for good every member of the body, and every faculty of the mind. It produces symmetry of character.

Holiness gives to its possessor control over all his bodily appetites. He has appetites. The Saviour, who was holiness itself in bodily form, had them. He was hungry and thirsty. The natural appetites were given us for a good purpose. They are not in themselves sinful. But they are to be kept within proper bounds. They were not intended to be our masters. They must be regulated and controlled. They are to be brought into subjection to reason, to conscience and the word of God. No holy person can be under the dominion of appetite. He is delivered from this bondage.

One who is holy never indulges his appetites in an unlawful manner. He will starve before he will steal. "I know," says the Apostle, "both how to be abased, and I know how to abound, every where and in all things I am instructed both to be full and to be hungry; both to abound and to suffer need."—Phil. 4:12. The Saviour, when he was hungry after having fasted forty days, would not obtain bread in the manner suggested by the devil. We should follow this example. No matter how strong may be the cravings of appetite, or to what straits we may be reduced, we should remember that there is something more to be considered than simply whether what is presented will assuage hunger, or satisfy thirst. Have I the right to it? Can I obtain the right on conditions with which I may lawfully comply? Esau did not steal, but he sold his birthright to obtain means to gratify his hunger. Many do the same to-day. The bodily appetites clamor for indulgence. Satan offers to gratify them on condition of some service rendered to him,—as breaking the Sabbath, catering to the vices of others, preaching the Gospel in such a manner as to throw out of sight the cross and the self-denial. A holy person will suffer the pangs of hunger before he will obtain his bread by any of these methods. If he will not resort to these means to keep from starving, of course he will not for any other purpose.

True holiness will give one such control over his appetites that he will not indulge them in an inordinate degree. He eats to live, but does not live to eat. His tastes are simple and natural.

CONTROL OF APPETITES.

His wants are easily satisfied. He who spends large sums of money to gratify his own pampered tastes, while so many are perishing of want, may be orthodox and polite, but he is not holy. No matter though he can afford to be "clothed in purple and fine linen, and fare sumptuously every day," yet he sees representatives of Christ in the destitute around him, and he denies himself of luxuries that he may minister to their necessities. Church festivals, to raise money, are open to this, among other objections. They educate the people to make self-gratification a stronger motive to action than duty to God, and to our fellow men. They assume that Christians will do more for their stomachs' sake than they will for conscience' sake. They take it for granted that they care more for their own sensual enjoyment, than they do for the claims of God, or the sufferings of their fellow men.

True holiness saves those who enjoy it from all unnatural, depraved appetites which have been formed by a course of sinful indulgence. Such is man's depravity that he forms appetites at which his physical nature at first revolts. After a while the indulgence of these appetites is attended with momentary enjoyment. Such is the use of opium, tobacco and ardent spirits. No one likes them at first. They frequently make beginners sick. But they stimulate the nervous system, and create an excitement which affords a certain degree of pleasure. When this excitement passes off, it is followed by a corresponding degree of languor and depression. This soon becomes so insupportable that the stimulant must be had at any cost. An appetite is formed that the victims will gratify at the expense of every thing which men hold dear. Property, friends, reputation, standing, health, and even life itself are sacrificed to gratify an appetite which brutalizes and enslaves. The only safe course is to avoid the beginning. But for those who sincerely repent of their wickedness in forming and feeding such an appetite, God provides a remedy. The promise, "If we confess our sins he is faithful and just to forgive us our sins and to cleanse us from all unrighteousness," (I John 1:9), covers this ground. The appetite for either of the stimulants named, cannot be godly—this no one contends. It cannot be indifferent,—it is of too positive a character. It is an unrighteousness,—both its nature and its effects proclaim this. That it is true of the appetite for opium and the appetite for ardent spirits is generally conceded. No one will maintain that a drunkard is holy. This ye know, that no drunkard shall inherit the kingdom of God. (I Cor. 10:6.) But an habitual tobacco user is as clearly condemned by the Scriptures, as is the one who habitually uses ardent spirits as a beverage. His habit involves, of necessity, personal filthiness. But we are commanded to cleanse ourselves from all filthiness of the flesh, and of the Spirit, perfecting holiness in the fear of the Lord. We readily admit that the works of holiness may be begun in the heart of a person who uses tobacco. But it cannot go on and this habit continue. One or the other will cease. He will cease to advance in holiness, or he will abandon his unholy habits. No person can perfect holiness without cleansing himself from all filthiness of the flesh, as well as of the Spirit.

Again, we are commanded to eat and drink to the glory of God. (I Cor. 10:31.) We do this when we eat temperately, and such things as do not injure us or others. But it is a fact, as clearly established as any fact can be, that the habitual use of tobacco breaks down the nervous system, and brings on many diseases. No man, immoderately addicted to the use of tobacco, can retain his mental vigor, and his bodily soundness, as he could without it. No one, seeing a professed Christian smoking or chewing, will think any more highly of the Christian religion on that account. It is an act, to say the least, in which God is not glorified.

No man has the right to spend the Lord's money in this way. It is God who gives the power to get wealth. It should be used to advance His cause,—to make men better,—to relieve their wants and instruct them in the way of life. A Christian man cannot spend his money as he wills, but must use it as the Lord wills.

But there is little use in multiplying words on this subject. Those who are really in earnest to gain Heaven, and who are willing to meet the conditions of salvation, cannot fail to see the necessity of denying themselves of the gratification of an appetite formed in sin, the indulgence of which can do no good, but must eventually result in much harm. Those who make religion a mere matter of convenience, or fashion, would not be convinced any way, and it would do no good if they were. It is useless to talk against idols, to men who are joined to their idols. But to those who have formed this appetite, and wish to be delivered from it, we say—holiness will do it. Seek earnestly to be delivered from bondage to your animal nature, and you shall be delivered. You will become spiritual by becoming holy. "As many as are led by the Spirit of God, they are the sons of God."—Rom. 8:14.

But if you are a slave to your appetites, do not profess holiness. If you do, you have no reason to expect that your profession will be received. Holiness is a radical work. It changes us in our appetites. The things that we once loved we now hate. Old things are passed away and behold all things are become new.

Give yourself no rest until this thorough work

is wrought in you. Seek to have the blood of cleansing applied to every part of your nature. Look to be sanctified wholly, and believe that—" Faithful is he that calleth you who also will do it."—I Thess. 5:24.

CHAPTER VIII.

ATTRIBUTES OF HOLINESS.—LOVE.

HOLINESS implies deliverance from all hatred of any human being. Personal enmities—either open or avowed, or subtle and secret—have a place, to a greater or less extent, in the hearts of men generally. Professing Christians scarcely form an exception. One interferes with our plans and purposes, and defeats our projects. As long as any selfishness remains in the soul, dislike is sure to follow. His actions are commented upon with severity, an unfavorable construction is put upon whatever he does and says, until he comes to be regarded with feelings of positive aversion. A truly sanctified soul has no sympathy with sin,—he abhors it; but he looks upon the sinner with sincere compassion.

In this respect, the supernatural character of Christianity is manifested. It is natural to return hatred for hatred. But holiness causes one to return good for evil, blessing for cursing, love for hatred. The teachings of Christ on this point are plain and unequivocal.—"Ye have heard that it hath been said, Thou shalt love thy neighbor, and hate thine enemy. But I say unto you, Love your enemies, bless them that curse you, do good to them that hate you, and pray for them that despitefully use you, and persecute you; That ye may be the children of your Father which is in heaven; for he maketh his sun to rise on the evil and on the good, and sendeth his rain on the just and on the unjust. For if you love them which love you, what reward have ye? do not even the publicans the same? And if ye salute your brethren only, what do ye more than others? Do not even the publicans so? Be ye therefore perfect, even as your Father which is in heaven is perfect."—Matt. 5:43-48.

This implies deliverance from all active hostility. It is deserving of notice that when the Apostle prays for the sanctification of believers, his prayer is addressed to the God of peace. "And the very God of peace sanctify you wholly."—I Thess. 5:23. The *God of peace* never gives the spirit of war. Whoever He sanctifies is made partaker of His peace. All animosities are buried.—Old enmities are forgotten. If you are thus made holy, you will forgive those who have wronged you. And what is still harder, you forgive those whom you have wronged. Instead of attempting to justify yourself by making them appear, both to yourself and others, as bad as possible, you take the blame to yourself, and confess it, and make everything right as far as it is in your power to do so. While you are by no means cowardly, you are no longer full of fight. You do not avail yourself of every opportunity to assail others when it can apparently be done to advantage. You do not strive for the mastery over others. If they assail you the assault is not returned. You do not return railing for railing, but contrariwise, blessing.

A holy person is saved from that modification of hatred usually denominated *prejudice*. It matters not whether it be individual, sectarian, or national, holiness removes it from the heart. At a camp-meeting which we attended, a young lady at the opening of the meeting, made a clear profession of holiness. She was active, but not forward. The light shone clearly, and she welcomed the light. In a short time she was among the most earnest seekers of a clean heart. She felt right in every particular but one. She had a prejudice against her step-mother, whom she had said she never would like.—But when the blessing came, it removed this feeling entirely. There was none of it left. She was willing to reciprocate the love which had been proffered her from one whom she ought to love.

A young man who had warmly espoused the Southern cause, and served in the Southern army, became convicted for the blessing of holiness from reading some numbers of THE EARNest Christian, which providentially fell into his hands. He sought and found full salvation through the blood of the Lamb. At a large, outdoor meeting, where hundreds were assembled, he felt called to confess what God had done for him. Among other things, he said that holiness took away all prejudice against the Yankees. This was said, not only at the risk of his personal popularity, but at the risk of his life. But he had to make and stand by the declaration.

At one of our large meetings in Western New York, a stranger arose and said he was a preacher from the central part of the State. He said he had heard a great many things against this people, but was determined to know about them for himself. Such was the prejudice, that he did not dare to let his nearest friends—not even his wife —know *where* he was going. "But," said he, "I am satisfied that God is with you. If any Christian comes among you, he is sure to love you. If he would keep up his prejudices, he must stay away and hate you."

Another modification of hatred is *envy*. This is a malignant feeling toward others because of their prosperity. It manifests itself in little things—such as detracting from the merits of others; making efforts to impair their reputation; attributing their success to anything that looks plausible, rather than to their own good conduct. This spirit is often manifested among professed Christians, ministers not excepted. They cannot bear to hear their rival well spoken of. But holiness takes this feeling away. We can rejoice with those that do rejoice.

Many are not saved from their enmities, because they do not want to be. They hold on to their prejudices as they would to life itself. Yet they profess holiness! Such persons are evidently deceived. There can be no mistake in the matter. They need to have the Lord circumcise their hearts. They are holding on to that which will work their ruin. "A little leaven leaveneth the whole lump." If grace does not root out malice, malice will kill out grace. The two cannot live together.

"But now ye also put off all these, anger, wrath, malice, filthy communication out of your mouth."—Col. 3:8.

CHAPTER IX.

ATTRIBUTES OF HOLINESS.—HATRED OF SIN.

HOLINESS is not indifference. One who is truly holy does not feel that he has done his duty by simply abstaining from sin. True holiness is not that easy, good-natured disposition that smiles at sin, and gives it ample toleration, especially if it is fashionable or popular, or capable of being turned to account in "building up the church," that is, adding to its numbers or influence. There was a great deal of this spurious kind of holiness in this country in the palmy days of slavery. You may search volume after volume of its literature, designed for circulation in the South, without finding one bold, manly, outspoken denunciation of the sin of slave-holding. You might have attended the "holiness meeting," week after week, without hearing one prayer offered for the liberation of the slave, or one testimony borne against the "sum of all villainies." No farther south than the city of New York, at no later a date than soon after President Lincoln's emancipation proclamation, you might have heard a brother called to order in the leading "holiness meeting" for thanking God for this proclamation which struck the fetters from three millions of bondmen.

The same kind of holiness is popular to-day. It valorously kicks the dead lion, but is very careful not to excite the anger of the living jackal. It hardly gives a passing notice to some of the greatest obstacles to the work of holiness in this country. If it mentions them, it is done so faintly as scarcely to attract attention. If it objects to them, it is in such weak tones as not to displease their most ardent votaries. We have attended a holiness camp-meeting without hearing one word said in condemnation of the practice, now so common among professed Christians, of adorning themselves "in gold and pearls and costly array." Everything was said in commendation of the beauty of holiness and of its exalting influence upon human character, but nothing to show the incongruity with it, of that pride which the Bible so strongly condemns. It is no uncommon thing to see even advocates of holiness adorned in a style that would, fifty years ago, have excluded them from the Church whose interests they are now laboring so zealously to promote.

True holiness is not blind. It has eyes to see, and ears to hear. While not obtrusive, it is observing. If it does not act the part of a detective: it does not assume the ignorance of an accessory. While not skeptical, it is not credulous. It does not call every thing gold that glitters. It tries those who say they are Apostles, and readily consents to be tried in turn. It does not accept professions merely because the manners are pleasing, and the words are faultless.

Scriptural holiness implies hatred of sin. This is one of the points in which it differs from mere natural amiability. It is not that easy, good-nature that smiles at vices it would not itself commit. It offers a stern resistance to sin in all its guises. It stands like a rock against the popular waves of iniquity. It does not give place to the devil. Satan cannot have his way undisputed in the presence of holiness. It maintains its ground against all odds and under all circumstances. "The fear of the Lord is to hate evil."—Prov. 8:13. "Ye that love the Lord hate evil."—Ps. 97:10.

One who is truly holy hates the first appearance of sin in himself. His conscience is as quick as the apple of the eye. A sinful thought, even when suggested by Satan and instantly repelled by the mind, gives him more uneasiness than a sinful action did before his conscience was purged from dead works. The one evil which he dreads above all others is sin. He shuns it as he would the open pit to which it leads. He cries out with the Psalmist: "I hate every false way."—Ps. 119:104. And again, "I hate vain thoughts, but thy law do I love.—Ps. 119:113. So Bunyan truly says, "Where the grace of God is in the heart it shows itself by inclining the soul to abhor sin."

He hates sin in others. No matter with what talents, or accomplishments, or position it may be joined, he abhors it utterly. The popularity of the sinner does not mitigate the repugnance which he feels on account of his sins. There is no malice in his hatred, but the holy soul feels an instinctive aversion to sin, no matter how polished may be its appearance. "Do not I hate them, O Lord, that hate thee? and am not I grieved with those that rise up against thee? I hate them with perfect hatred: I count them mine enemies."—Ps. 139:21, 22. This does not imply angry, malevolent feelings, but a settled aversion of soul toward the haters of God. As to his chosen companions, the Psalmist says, "I am a companion of all them that fear thee, and of them that keep thy precepts."—Ps. 119:63.

Hatred of sin is essential to the aggressiveness that belongs to the Christian character. No disciple of Christ can settle down, and enjoy himself, without making any effort to do good to others. He that has found Christ will proclaim Christ. "Let him that heareth say, Come."—Rev. 22:17. "He that is not with me is against me; and he that gathereth not with me scattereth abroad."—Matt. 12:30. But unless one feels a hatred to sin he will not make war upon sin. A man who goes to the bar and drinks water, while his friend drinks whiskey may be personally temperate; but he certainly cannot be a very warm advocate of temperance. It was when Paul saw that the city was wholly given, to idolatry that his spirit was stirred within him, and he preached to them the true and living God. Luther would never have been a reformer, had not his indignation been aroused against the sinful practices of the Church. He made war upon the sale of indulgences because he hated the sins that were thus encouraged. One who sees little or no harm in pride will not insist upon humility. He who thinks that a conspiracy of the strong against the weak, the union of believers with unbelievers, cemented by the most awful oaths and penalties, is a matter of so little importance as not to be worthy to be looked into, will not oppose secret societies with any earnestness.

So of sin in all its manifestations; until it is seen to be "*exceeding sinful*," and hateful, no vigorous effort will be made for its overthrow. Revivals will dwindle down into periodical efforts to promote the interests of each particular sect, and the converts, instead of being made happy in God, will become at best only the zealous proselytes of the favorite opinion.

Hatred of sin will necessarily expose a person to persecution. It cannot be otherwise. Satan will never surrender without a struggle. If he is attacked he will attack in turn. He will return blow for blow. He has no scruples and feels no pity. No lie, if only it is clothed with probability, will be too great or glaring for him to employ. No character can be too well established for him to assail. When he cannot use violence he will make the most of defamation; of all the arts of which he is a most consummate master. He is ever the relentless enemy of all good. Hence the Apostle declares, "Yea, and all that will live godly in Christ Jesus shall suffer persecution."—II Tim. 3:12. This is a general declaration. It applies to all time and all places. It must hold good as long as holiness is opposed to sin. No degree of wisdom or prudence can enable one to escape this consequence of a godly life. If you have met with no persecution it is an alarming symptom. It shows that there is an essential element wanting in your religious experience. You do not hate sin.

Hatred to sin secures the comfort of the Holy Ghost. There is no joy like that which He imparts.

> "A peace to sensual minds unknown,
> A joy unspeakable."

With this in the heart one can go through any thing that in the Providence of God he is called upon to suffer or endure. "The joy of the Lord is your strength." Yet many professed Christians know nothing about this joy. They have never felt it themselves and when they witness it in others it looks to them like fanaticism or wild-fire. The reason they have never felt it is, they have never been sufficiently given up to God to obey Him in every thing, to secure the comfort of the Holy Ghost. "Thou lovest righteousness, and hatest wickedness; therefore God, thy God, hath anointed thee with the oil of gladness above thy fellows."—Ps. 45:7. Heb. 1:9. To be "anointed with the oil of gladness" it is not enough to love righteousness. If you stop there you will not receive it. You must go a step farther and become a *partaker* of so much of *the divine nature* as will make you *hate wickedness*. Then, when you take your stand against it; when you meet, unmoveable as a rock, the billows of wickedness, God will pour upon you the oil of gladness to that degree that you will not heed the sufferings you will endure for your fidelity to Christ. You will have the martyr spirit.

Hatred to sin will enable you to stand true to God under all circumstances. You will not backslide. As long as sin looks odious you will not embrace it. While you fight sin in real earnest, *because it is sin against God*, you will not become its friend. It is the half-hearted renunciation of sin which causes so many to fall away. Lot, in Sodom, maintained his integrity because "in seeing and hearing, he vexed his righteous soul from day to day with their unlawful deeds." —II Pet. 2:8.

CHAPTER X.

ATTRIBUTES OF HOLINESS.—HONESTY IN BUSINESS.

HONESTY is that disposition which prompts us to give to every one his due. It makes us thoughtful of the rights of others. Its influence is felt in all the relations of life. It makes us more anxious to give to others their rights, than we are to insist upon our own. We would infinitely prefer to be the victims of injustice, than to be unjust. A holy person would a thousand times rather suffer wrong, than do wrong. He watches carefully lest others be the losers through his fault. He never takes advantage of the ignorance of another. In buying, he does not decry an article in order to obtain it for less than it is worth : in selling, he does not conceal defects in order to obtain more for a thing than its real value. He freely gives all the information necessary to form a correct judgment in the matter. Even the heathen standard of honesty did not allow one man to take advantage of the ignorance of another. Cicero proposes a case as follows. He says, "Antisthenes brings a ship-load of grain to Rhodes at a time of great scarcity. The Rhodians flock about him to buy. He knows that five other ships, laden with grain, will be there to-morrow. Ought he to tell the Rhodians this, before he sells his own grain? Undoubtedly he ought, otherwise he makes a gain of their ignorance, and so is no better than a thief or a robber." You may say, "Business is business, and religion is religion," but that does not relieve the matter. The Bible demands honesty in business. A holy man regulates and controls his business according to the principles of justice. Yet many who profess the holy religion of Jesus purposely take advantage of the ignorance of others, and so " are no better than thieves and robbers."

One takes advantage of the necessities of others. Some labor must be done, or service performed. The want is urgent. Yet he who takes advantage of this necessity and extorts an unreasonable price for the service rendered, acts precisely upon the principle of the highwayman who takes advantage of the traveller's helpless condition and demands his money or his life. When we undertake to assist another, though there be no stipulation as to the compensation to be received, our obligations to God will not allow us to be unreasonable in our requirements. We must do as we would be done by.

Holiness implies honesty between employers and the employed. If I sell my time and skill to another ; to fail in rendering him the service for which I am paid, is, as really an act of dishonesty as to rob his till, or steal his goods. So the apostle commands those who are working for others to do it "in singleness of your heart, as unto Christ; not with eye-service, as menpleasers; but as the servants of Christ, doing the will of God from the heart; with good will doing service, as to the Lord, and not to men: knowing that whatsoever good thing any man doeth, the same shall he receive of the Lord."—Eph. 6:6.

The employers are to give servants their due, not taking advantage of their wants and getting their service for less than its value; nor paying them in that which they do not want. An eminent minister hired a young man to work for him through the season. When they settled the minister gave him his note. This was satisfactory at the time. But circumstances soon after rendered it necessary for the young man to return to his friends quite a distance away. The minister, as the expression is, *shaved his own note*. As far as honesty is concerned he might as well have stolen from him that amount.

In the family relations, in the every day occurrences of life, there is need for the constant exercise of this principle. We must "follow holiness, without which no man shall see the Lord," not only in the Church, but in the family, in the treatment of companion, and children, and dependents, in the workshop and on the farm, behind the counter and in the office, in meeting obligations and in making bargains, on the streets and in the cars, and in all our intercourse with our fellow-men.

CHAPTER XI.

ATTRIBUTES OF HOLINESS.—IMPARTIALITY.

GOD is no respecter of persons. This does not mean that He regards the righteous and the wicked with the same degree of favor. But it does mean that He loves a poor man who is truly pious, just as much as He does a millionaire or a king who serves Him no better. In the ranks of an army, in time of war, are men from every position in life; but there are for all the same duties and the same dangers. The road to preferment is open to all alike. What is true, in theory at least, in the army, is true in fact in the Church of Jesus Christ. The same spirit of obedience and self-renunciation is required of all. "So whosoever of you he be, that forsaketh not all that he hath, he cannot be my disciple," (Luke 14:33), was not spoken to those only who have not much to forsake. It applies with equal force to the prince as to the pauper.

In proportion as we become holy we become partakers of the mind that was in Christ. A holy person will not claim, and *will not accept* any privilege in the house of God which is conceded to him on account of his wealth, but is denied to his poor but equally deserving brother. To him there is a depth of meaning in the words of our Saviour; "How can ye believe which receive honor one of another, and seek not the honor that cometh from God only?"—John 5:44. He is "a companion"—an equal—"of all them that fear God," (Ps. 119:63), and he does not accept any honor bestowed upon him on account of the superior worldly advantages he may enjoy.

Consequently a holy person should not buy or rent a seat in a house of worship. To do this would be to give his sanction to a practice which shuts the poor out of the house of God, and which introduces into the Church an aristocracy based on money.

Christ says, "The poor have the Gospel preached to them."—Matt. 11:5. This is the standing miracle of the Gospel. False religions seek their votaries among the rich and powerful. The Gospel was made for the poor. It is adapted to their capacities and their wants. If the rich receive it they must come down to a level with the poor. They must lay aside their "gold and pearls and costly array" and be clothed upon with humility. In all ages the greatest triumphs of the Gospel have been won among the poor. Paul, writing to the saints at Corinth, one of the proudest cities of his times, said, "Ye see your calling, brethren, how that not many

IMPARTIALITY.

wise men after the flesh, not many mighty, not many noble are called; but God hath chosen the foolish things of the world to confound the wise; and God hath chosen the weak things of the world to confound the things which are mighty; and base things of the world, and things which are despised hath God chosen, yea, and things which are not, to bring to nought things that are."—I Cor. 1:26-28.

John Wesley commenced his wonderful career among the poor, and his followers were mainly of this class. Were the churches holy, their houses of worship would be open for the poor just as freely as for the rich, and there would be one communion for all; as there is one God and Father of us all. An individual who is holy cannot consistently belong to a Church that despises the poor. But if grading a congregation according to its wealth—giving to the one, who is able and willing to pay the most, the best seat, irrespective of his Christian, or even moral character, and giving the poor seats by themselves, is not manifesting contempt for the poor, we know not how it can be manifested in the house of God. True holiness would correct all this. It honors those whom God honors. It would make trouble, for those professing holiness to refuse to give their sanction to the selling of the right to hear the Gospel. But this is the nature of holiness to make trouble wherever it comes in contact with sin. Light has no communion with darkness, and where one prevails it is to the exclusion of the other.

God has nowhere promised that holy men should enjoy exemption from troubles. But they are promised a final and glorious deliverance.

If you steadfastly refuse to show respect of persons in judgment, you may bring upon yourself persecution; but in no other way can you keep clear in your soul. There is a sterling integrity about holiness, which refuses to be swerved from righteous judgment by any apprehension of danger or expectation of reward. It chooses to "suffer affliction with the people of God, rather than to enjoy the pleasures of sin for a season."—Heb. 11:25. Job says, "The cause which I knew not I searched out." He did not accept the popular voice as his verdict. He examined carefully, weighed impartially the evidence, and gave a just decision. "Thou shalt not respect the person of the poor, nor honor the person of the mighty: but in righteousness shalt thou judge thy neighbor."—Lev. 19:15.

CHAPTER XII.

ATTRIBUTES OF HOLINESS.—LOVE TO GOD.

THERE can be no such thing as Christian holiness without supreme love to God. This is its very substance. It may be summed up in this. A being possessed of the proper intelligence, and actuated at all times by supreme love to God, would never be wanting in any duty. Every obligation would be fulfilled. The GREAT COMMANDMENT is, "Thou shalt love the Lord thy God with all thy heart, and with all thy soul, and with all thy mind."—Matt. 22:37. A failure here involves failure everywhere. Who is pleased with professions of love when convinced that the affection is wanting? So Christ assures us that acts of devotion are unutterably loathsome unless they spring from love. "So then because thou art lukewarm, and neither cold nor hot, I will spew thee out of my mouth." —Rev. 3:16.

Love to God does not differ in its nature from love to our fellows. The more pure are our conceptions of the object of our affections, the more exalted is the sentiment. God is infinite in all the wonderful attributes of His nature; and hence, love to Him is the most exalted and ennobling affection of which the human mind is capable. It includes delight in Him, desire to enjoy His presence and His approbation, and a determination to do His will. "For this is the love of God, that we keep his commandments." —I John 5:3.

It is manifested by a desire to please Him. Anything we feel satisfied will be pleasing to God, we are anxious to do, although it may involve painstaking and self-denial. David's men loved him; and when he expressed a longing for water from a well which was within the lines of the enemy, and carefully guarded, they sallied forth, and sword in hand, obtained it at the risk of their lives. So one who truly loves God, will rejoice at any intimation of his ability to perform any service acceptable to Him. Many of the martyrs went rejoicing to the stake, because an opportunity was given them to demonstrate to the world that the love of God is stronger than the love of life. He who chooses a religious life because, instead of its being attended with any serious interference with his love of ease, and of worldly pleasures, and of worldly popularity, it will add to his reputation among men, is utterly wanting in the very first element of a holy character. Unless our first aim is to please God, we need inquire no farther. There is a fundamental lack. She who puts on apparel to please men rather than God should make no pretensions to sanctity. There can be none. To profess it is absurd.

He who truly loves God will honestly and carefully endeavor to ascertain His will. "O how I love thy law! it is my meditation all the day."—Ps. 119:97. And again, "Thy word have I hid in mine heart, that I might not sin against thee. I have rejoiced in the way of thy testimonies, as much as in all riches. I will meditate in thy precepts, and have respect unto thy ways."—Ps. 119:11, 14, 15. This is the language of one who loves God. He studies the Bible— not as a literary critic, but with a sincere desire to know the will of God concerning him. There was never a saint who did not love the word of God. The knowledge that a holy person desires above all other, is a knowledge of God's will. So he studies the sacred writings—not to establish a doctrine or prove a disputed point; but to really find out what God requires of him. He would not pervert it, nor make it bend to his convenience or his prejudices. But let one lose the love of God out of his heart, and the relish for the Bible is gone. It is generally neglected. If read, as it may be when the light becomes darkness, it is that its meaning may be perverted so as to form an excuse for an unholy life. There are many now, as in the Apostle's day, "who handle the word of God deceitfully."

A holy person has his ear open to the voice of God in the soul. There is a still, small voice, that one who loves God does not fail to hear. He who formed the ear can speak to the ear. In many things respecting which the word of God is silent, or speaks only in general terms, we need specific directions by the Holy Spirit. "As many as are led by the Spirit of God they are the sons of God."—Rom. 8:14. If we love God, we delight to hear Him speak to us. Even if reproof is given, we rejoice to hear it. We are glad to listen even to the warnings that our Heavenly Father gives. But his voice of approbation compensates a thousand times for any hardships we may have undergone, or any sacrifices we may have made. In whatever way God speaks, or whatever may be the import of His message, He always finds in those who love Him attentive listeners. They are so thankful for the condescension showed that they listen with the utmost reverence and attention. In their hearts they say, "Speak, Lord, for thy servant heareth."

The truly devout also take delight in ascertaining the will of God as shown in the physical laws by which our bodies and other material substances are governed. A lover of God is likely to be a lover of nature.

If we love God we have a high relish for that

preaching and that reading which most plainly discloses, and most strongly enforces the will of God. We try those who say they are apostles. It was to embodied spirits,—to preachers and teachers of the Gospel—that the Apostle refers when he says, "Beloved, believe not every spirit, but try the spirits whether they are of God:" for he assigns as a reason, "because many false prophets are gone out into the world."—I John 4:1. We shall hear and support preachers—not because they are talented or eloquent—but because they speak the word of God faithfully. This will be to us of prime importance. No amount of polished oratory will be accepted as a substitute for fidelity to God. A holy person cannot give encouragement to compromisers and trimmers. He cannot bid them God-speed who bring another Gospel. He does not help false prophets—no matter though they may belong to his own denomination—by giving them his presence and his money. This, again, will make trouble. But holiness, in a sinful world, has always been a troublesome thing. It is so because it is holiness.

Again, if we love God we shall manifest it by unquestioning obedience to all His commands. There can be no real love to God without the spirit of obedience. Our Saviour makes obedience the test of love. "He that hath my commandments, and keepeth them, he it is that loveth me; and he that loveth me shall be loved of my Father, and I will love him and will manifest myself to him."—John 14:21. This is clear and conclusive. Professions of love to God, when attended by manifest disobedience to His commands, show how easy it is to be deceived. Christ cannot be mistaken; but the most intelligent among us may be very much out of the way, especially in the opinion which we entertain of our own state of grace. We are safe only as we measure ourselves by the standard which God gives. And He repeatedly gives obedience as the test of love.

We must have respect to all of His commands. It will not do for us to make choice of those which it is fashionable to obey, and disregard those that are commonly disregarded. Such a course would prove that we are the slaves of fashion, instead of being the servants of God. This was what brought upon the Pharisees the severest denunciations the Saviour ever uttered.

Finally, he who loves God has a spirit of devotion. He loves the worship of God, secret, social and public. The saints have always been a praying people. They talk a great deal to God. If they cannot use the enticing words of man's wisdom, they can plead before the throne with "groanings that cannot be uttered," and their prayers avail. They know that they have the things they ask for. They love the mercy-seat. Those who have been mighty on earth for God, were mighty in prayer. David was a valiant warrior; but his fiercest battles were fought out in his closet. Elijah was too strong for his king, had power over the elements, and openly conquered death, because he prevailed in prayer.

Prayer answered turns to praise.—Hence one who loves God delights in His praises. With the Psalmist he says, "I will bless the Lord at all times: his praise shall continually be in my mouth."—Ps. 34:1. See how full the Psalms are of the praises of God. In the New Testament we are commanded to "rejoice in the Lord always." Now if we love God, we shall delight to do this. We would as soon think of hiring others to eat our necessary food for us, as to hire them to praise God for us while our own tongues are silent. A holy people will never employ others to worship God for them! Never!—Acts of worship performed by the ungodly or indifferent, even though they be done decently and in order, and paid for by the church, are but open mockery and not worship. Mere sound, though it be pleasant to the ear, is not worship. "God is a Spirit: and they that worship him must worship him in spirit and in truth."—John 4:24.

CHAPTER XIII.

ATTRIBUTES OF HOLINESS.—TRUST IN GOD.

TRUE holiness brings man into the most intimate relations with His Creator. He is *a child of God.* Of this he is assured by the direct witness of the Spirit. Those terms which express the greatest solicitude which one human being can feel in another, are employed to represent the care which our Heavenly Father has over those who walk before Him in the beauty of holiness. Can any thing exceed the care which a father has for a son whom he tenderly loves? How he endeavors to give him the education which will best fit him for the duties of life! What self-denial does he often practice that this may be accomplished! How he watches over his disposition, and labors to correct his faults! How he warns him against such associations as may work to his injury! But God says, "I will be a Father unto you, and ye shall be my sons and daughters, saith the Lord Almighty."—II Cor. 6:18. Yet the love of a mother, if not stronger, is more enduring than a father's love. It follows her child with cease-

TRUST IN GOD.

less anxiety to the ends of the earth, and to the close of life. It survives the loss of character, and the wreck of hope. It goes, with tearful eye and ardent sympathy, and trembling step, with the criminal to his cell, and the murderer to the gallows. But a mother may forget her child, but God will never forget those who separate themselves to His service. They are said to be graven upon the palms of His hands to be continually before Him.

A holy person, then, trusts in God. All his interests, for time and eternity, are committed to the keeping of Him who never wearies. He has confidence in God. A loving child is not always exacting promises—he trusts his parents for all his needs. So a holy person trusts in God himself. He has confidence in the ability and in the willingness of His Heavenly Father to do for him the very best that his circumstances call for. He may not always see how it is coming out. He does not ask to. He feels the utmost assurance that all things work together for good to them that love God. With that he is satisfied.

He trusts God in particular:

For all the grace that he needs. He knows that God can carry him through. The channel supplied from a mighty river, may be small but it is always full. The source of the supply is inexhaustible. So is it with the fountain of all goodness. There is grace for us for any emergency. We never need be overcome. No matter how sudden may be the attack, our Protector is ever at hand. The darts thrown at us may be fiery, and hurled with tremendous force, but they can never penetrate our shield. The enemies that assail us may be legion, but more are they that are for us. Thus a holy person, while not presumptuous, is confident in God. He knows in whom he trusts, and that He is able to keep, in perfect security, that which He has committed to His care. Whatever may be his duties, whatever God may call upon him to do, He will give him grace to perform. Increasing loads of care, and labor, and responsibility may be laid upon him, but his strength is so multiplied that he is able always to testify that Christ's yoke is easy, and His burden light. Temptations most furious, most subtle, and nicely adapted to accomplish their end may assail him, but he always finds that with the temptation, God provides a way of escape, that he may be able to bear it. So his confidence in God that He will give him increased strength, as his wants require, never fails. He is not discouraged, ever ready to give up the battle; but he boldly renews it from time to time, and goes in for new conquests, and an extension of Christ's kingdom. He knows that the battle is the Lord's, and he never expects defeat.

He trusts God for temporal blessings. If God is the giver of every good and perfect gift, we should naturally expect that He would provide for His children. So His word declares that He will "withhold no good thing from them that walk uprightly." He knows best what is good for us. We take the remedies which a doctor in whom we have confidence prescribes, without knowing before hand what their effects may be ; and shall we not as cheerfully accept from our Father's hand whatever temporal dispensations He may order ? Disappointment may be bitter, but it may be just the remedy we need to sharpen the appetite for spiritual food. Toils and privations may be grievous to the flesh, but they may be necessary to purify our spirits of their grossness and fit them for their upward flight. But whatever is best God will give us if we walk before Him in the light of holiness. Every holy person has the most unbounded confidence in the declaration, "Seek ye first the kingdom of God, and his righteousness ; and all these things shall be added unto you."—Matt. 6:33. This does not make him indolent or improvident. Quite the contrary. He labors unweariedly because he labors in hope. He is "not slothful in business, fervent in spirit, serving the Lord."— Rom. 12:11. He does the best he can, dismisses all anxiety, and commits all to the hands of God, for soul and body, for time and eternity.

He who can trust God for his happiness in another world, certainly can have no hesitation in trusting Him to have his necessary wants supplied for the few fleeting years of his probationary existence. If God cares for the oxen, and cares for the grass of the field, He will care for His children. Their wants will be provided for if they do their duty. He can send manna in the desert, and bring water from the flinty rock. So a holy person rests in the promise, "Your bread shall be given you, and your water shall be sure." His Protector is always at hand: his Provider is always near. The Lord is his refuge: the Most High is his habitation. "They that trust in the Lord shall be as Mount Zion which cannot be removed, but abideth forever."—Ps. 125:1.

CHAPTER XIV.

ATTRIBUTES OF HOLINESS.—LOVE OF MAN.

WE have seen that there can be no true holiness without the love of God. Neither can there be without love for our fellow men. The two are joined together. The second great commandment is, "Thou shalt love thy neighbor as thyself."—Matt. 22:39. Our Saviour, in the account which he gives of the good Samaritan, (Luke 10:30), teaches us that our neighbor is any one, even though belonging to an unfriendly nation, who stands in need of our sympathy and assistance. A holy person feels a lively interest in the well-being of his fellow men. His heart is large—it takes in mankind. His arms are long—they carry assistance to the perishing in the ends of the earth. He enters into the spirit of the great commission, "Go ye into all the world and preach the Gospel to every creature."—Mark 16:15. His law knows no boundary lines. His efforts to do good are not confined to any territorial limits. His righteousness goeth forth "as a lamp that burneth."—Isa. 62:1.

In addition to active good-will towards all mankind, holiness implies a special love for our brethren, the children of God. The New Testament is very explicit on this point. "If a man say, I love God, and hateth his brother, he is a liar: for he that loveth not his brother whom he hath seen, how can he love God whom he hath not seen?"—I John 4:20. Comment can make these words no plainer. "We know that we have passed from death unto life, because we love the brethren."—I John 3:14. This love is not bare sentiment. It is an ardent affection. It makes us care for each other's interest and welfare. We take pleasure in each other's company, "not forsaking the assembling of ourselves together; . . . but exhorting one another daily."—Heb. 10:25. If one member suffer, all the members suffer with it. If one soul is in destitution, those who have, are ready to supply his necessities. "Whoso hath this world's good, and seeth his brother have need, and shutteth up his bowels of compassion from him, how dwelleth the love of God in him?"—I John 3:17. If one is in peril, others share his danger. This is the spirit of true holiness. It was exemplified fully in the primitive Christians. Paul says: "After ye were illuminated ye endured a great fight of afflictions; partly while ye were made a gazing-stock both by reproaches and afflictions; and partly while ye became companions of them that were so used. For ye had compassion of me in my bonds, and took joyfully the spoiling of your goods, knowing in yourselves that ye have in heaven a better and an enduring substance."—Heb. 10 : 32-34. Lucian, a Roman writer, says of the early Christians: "It is incredible what expedition they use when any of their friends are known to be in trouble. In a word, they spare nothing on such an occasion, —for those miserable men have no doubt they shall be immortal and live forever; therefore they contemn death and many surrender themselves to sufferings. Moreover, their first lawgiver has taught them they are all brethren, when once they have turned, and renounced the gods of the Greeks, and worship this Master of theirs who was crucified, and engage to live according to His laws. They have also a sovereign contempt for all the things of this world, and look upon them as common." This is the testimony borne by an enemy.

A holy person does not love indiscriminately and blindly those who profess to be Christians, simply because they belong to the same church that he does. This displays a partisan spirit. He tries those who say they are apostles. His love is not the result of any reasonings; nor is it based on natural qualities nor acquired gifts. It springs from the love of Christ. We love Him so greatly that we instinctively love His true friends. Those who walk in the light have fellowship for each other. They find each other out, and their hearts naturally run together.—Rays of light, coming from the same source, easily mingle. Living streams, however widely separated, unite at last in the ocean. Holy persons feel that union of spirit, which is properly called, the communion of saints.

Holiness implies love for our enemies. It is impossible to have true holiness without having enemies. Christ had them. He told His disciples they should have them. "If ye were of the world, the world would love his own; but because ye are not of the world, but I have chosen you out of the world, therefore the world hateth you."—John 15:19.

If you belong to Christ, His enemies will be your enemies. They will hate you. Their hostility will sometimes assume an active form. They will go just as far as the law will allow them to go in manifesting this hostility. They will traduce you, misrepresent your actions, and impugn your motives. But what must you do? Stand still and see the salvation of God. You must feel the compassion for them that you would for an insane person. Neglect no opportunity to do them good. Never get tried with them, nor attempt to repay them evil for evil. Our Saviour's command is very plain: "Love your enemies. Bless them that curse you; do good to them that hate you, and pray for them which despitefully use you and persecute you." —Matt. 5:44. This is Bible holiness. No other religion but that of Jesus will enable a person to do this. There may be the semblance. Anger may be suppressed by force of resolution. But God alone is able to make us really love our enemies, and honestly strive to promote their welfare. The Holy Spirit will enable us to hate sin, and love the sinner. It will make us kind to them, but not indulgent to their faults. Holiness is not blind. It has eyes as well as heart. It never mistakes darkness for light. To one who has true holiness it is not hard to obey the command, "If thine enemy hunger, feed him; if he thirst, give him drink; for in so doing thou shalt heap coals of fire on his head."—Rom. 12:20.

CHAPTER XV.

ATTRIBUTES OF HOLINESS.—JOY.

JOY forms an essential element of true holiness. As caloric pervades matter, so joy is interfused through every sanctified soul. It may be developed more on some occasions than on others but it is always there. Not that a saint of God is exempt from sorrows, but in the midst of sufferings he can say with the Apostle, "As sorrowful, yet always rejoicing."—II Cor. 6:10. Vessels floating on a river are driven up stream by the wind, but underneath, the current flows steadily on to the ocean. So the sad occurrences of life occasion grief to the saint, while down deep in the heart joy reigns undisturbed.

This joy is not of earthly origin. It does not stand connected with temporal prosperity. Prosperity does not create it; adversity does not destroy it. The good opinion of our fellow-men does not set it in motion, nor their persecutions stop its steady flow. It does not spring from the consciousness of the possession of any gifts, natural or gracious. It is supernatural in its origin; pure and holy in its nature. It comes from God as directly as pardon comes from God. It is imparted to the soul by the direct power of the Spirit. Hence it is called the joy of the Holy Ghost. That is, the joy which the Holy Ghost imparts. It is a God-given happiness—happiness intensified. It is not levity. It is a solid joy.

There is a strong tendency to undervalue this joy. It is spoken of frequently by professed Christians in a contemptuous manner, as emotional, affecting only weak-minded persons, and short-lived in its continuance. That it is emotional, we admit. So is the compassion which leads us to relieve the suffering, without which, we are as "sounding brass or a tinkling cymbal." —I Cor. 13:1. And whoever reads his Bible will find that some very strong-minded persons have been affected with joy to an overpowering degree. David was a mighty man. But so great was his gladness when the ark of the Lord was brought up into his city, that "he danced before the Lord with all his might." When his proud wife "saw King David leaping and dancing before the Lord, she despised him in her heart." (II Sam. 6:14, 16.) But God cursed her and blessed the king. As to its duration, holy joy is to last forever. "And the ransomed of the Lord shall return, and come to Zion with songs and everlasting joy upon their heads: they shall obtain joy and gladness, and sorrow and sighing shall flee away."—Isa. 35:10.

That this joy is an essential element of true

holiness, we prove from the Scriptures. "Thou hast made known to me the ways of life; thou shalt make me full of joy with thy countenance."—Acts 2:28. The way of life is a saving knowledge of God. A look of approbation from Him fills the soul with joy. "I will see you again, and your heart shall rejoice, and your joy no man taketh from you."—John 16:22. The disciples were sad at the prospect that Jesus was about to leave them. He consoled them with the promise that He would manifest Himself to them spiritually—would be with them always, and this would afford them a joy that no man could deprive them of. This joy is just as free for the disciples of Jesus now as it was then. More than this, it is positively promised. "He that hath my commandments and keepeth them, he it is that loveth me; and he that loveth me shall be loved of my Father, and I will love him, and will manifest myself to him."—John 14:21. Every holy soul obeys Christ, and so Christ gives him a joy that man cannot take from him.

"For the kingdom of God is not meat and drink, but righteousness, and peace and joy in the Holy Ghost."—Rom. 14:17. Here holiness is said to consist of three elements. We have just as much right to conclude that we have it when we are destitute of the righteousness as we have, when destitute of the joy. God has joined the three together. Let no man put them asunder.

"And the disciples were filled with joy and with the Holy Ghost."—Acts 13:52. This, too, was in the midst of a violent persecution. "The fruit of the Spirit is love, joy, peace, long-suffering, gentleness, goodness, faith, meekness, temperance."—Gal. 5:22. No one can have true holiness without having the Spirit of God. But wherever the Spirit of God is, it will bring forth its appropriate fruits,—not one, but all,—not in some favorite localities, merely,—but in all places—not occasionally, but constantly. Joy is just as really one of the fruits of the Spirit as love or peace. Whoever has the Spirit of God has joy.

"In whom though now ye see him not, yet believing ye rejoice with joy unspeakable and full of glory."—I Peter 1:8. Whoever enjoys true holiness is a believer in Jesus. But all believers have joy unspeakable and full of glory.

How explicit are the Scriptures on this point. They show plainly that wherever holiness is, there is joy. We might go on at an indefinite length, for the Scriptures are as full, as they are plain; but if these passages which we have quoted do not carry conviction, no amount of proof will avail. The difficulty is beyond the reach of argument—it lies in the heart and not in the intellect.

But we are not alone in our opinion of the teaching of the Bible in this matter. John Wesley says, "True religion, or a heart right towards God and man, implies happiness as well as holiness. It is not only righteousness, but also peace and joy in the Holy Ghost. Joy wrought in the heart by the Holy Ghost, by the ever blessed Spirit of God. * * * This peace, joy, love—this change from glory to glory is what the wisdom of the world has voted to be madness, mere enthusiasm, utter distraction. But thou, O man of God, regard them not; be thou moved by none of those things. See that no man take thy crown. * * * * *

"Joy in the Holy Ghost will far more effectually purify the soul, than the want of that joy; and the peace of God is the best means of refining the soul from the dross of earthly affections. * * Without doubt our joy in the Lord will increase as our love increases."

President Edwards was a rigid Calvinist—a man of gigantic intellect, great learning and solid piety. He says, "The Scriptures speak of holy joy, as a great part of true religion. So it is represented.

"And as an important part of religion, exhorted to and pressed with great earnestness. 'Delight thyself in the Lord, and he shall give thee the desires of thine heart.'—Ps. 37:4. 'Rejoice in the Lord ye righteous.'—Ps. 97:12. So, 'Rejoice in the Lord, O, ye righteous.'—Ps. 33:1. 'Rejoice and be exceeding glad.'—Matt. 5:12.

'Finally, my brethren, rejoice in the Lord.'— Phil. 3:1. 'Rejoice in the Lord alway; and again I say, Rejoice.'—Phil. 4:4. 'Rejoice evermore.' —I Thess. 5:16. 'Let Israel rejoice in him that made him; let the children of Zion be joyful in the King.'—Ps. 149:2. This is mentioned among the principal fruits of the Spirit of grace. (Gal. 5:22.) The Psalmist mentions his holy joy as an evidence of his sincerity. 'I have rejoiced in the way of thy testimonies as much as in all riches.'—Ps. 119:14.

"He who has no religious affection, is in a state of spiritual death, and is wholly destitute of the powerful, quickening, saving influences of the Spirit of God upon his heart."

The hymns that are sung by all denominations present precisely the view of joy as forming an essential element of true holiness which we have here set forth. In many a church they sing with Watts,

"The men of grace have found,
Glory begun below."

If glory is not begun in your heart, there is a serious lack in your experience. In like manner, we sing with Charles Wesley,

"How happy every child of grace,
Who knows his sins forgiven."

But similar sentiments are found in every orthodox hymn book. If they are not true, why sing them? Is it right to sing lies? If they are true, why settle down in your religious experience without this joy, as though an essential element of holiness were of no consequence? Many not only do this, but even oppose and persecute those who are enabled, through grace, to "rejoice with joy unspeakable and full of glory." —I Peter 1:8. Others who do not go so far, treat these rejoicing ones in a patronizing kind of way, as though they were to be tolerated and pitied. True holiness of itself will make its possessor happy and triumphant. His springs are in God, and they never run dry. He does not go to the world for pleasures, but is "abundantly satisfied with the fatness of God's house, and drinks of the rivers of his pleasure.—Ps. 36:8.

CHAPTER XVI.

EXAMPLES OF HOLINESS.

IT is easier to follow than to lead. Ordinary navigators can cross the ocean after Columbus has led the way. A few lessons from Morse enables one with common aptness to send a message a thousand miles in an instant of time. We do not wait, before we embark in any business enterprise which we think will be greatly to our advantage, until everybody else has gone into it; but if it commends itself to our judgment, and a single individual, with no advantages superior to our own, has achieved a marked success, we press boldly forward.

Why should we not do so in religious experience? Why run a greater hazard for the gold that perisheth than for the gold tried in the fire? Why press on with the multitude in the broad way, strewed with wrecks of early hopes, and which ends in darkness and destruction? Why neglect the narrow way, which a few have demonstrated is not only feasible, but increasingly delightful, until it takes us where there are pleasures for evermore?

In all ages, there have been those who have experienced the blessing of holiness in their hearts and exemplified it in their lives. They have not been the honored of earth. Generally they were persecuted and despised while living. Their true characters were understood and appreciated by but few. But they have left an example which will shine with increasing lustre to the latest generations.

ABEL leads the van of the blood-washed army. We know but little about him. But this we are told, that he did not rely upon his natural goodness, but came to God through faith in the atoning blood. He brought of the firstlings of his flock. His offering spoke of his sense of sinfulness, of his penitence, and of his acceptance of the great truth that "without shedding of blood there is no remission of sins." He found favor and acceptance with God, and died the death of a martyr. "By faith Abel offered unto God a more excellent sacrifice than Cain, by which he obtained witness that he was righteous, God testifying of his gifts: and by it he being dead yet speaketh."—Heb, 11:4.

ENOCH. He was the seventh from Adam. In what respect those times were more favorable for living a godly life than the present, we are at a loss to imagine. If the world had not had as long an experience in wickedness, neither had it in goodness. There was no written revelation of

God's will.—The countless examples which we have of the ruinous effects of sin, and of the advantages of holiness, were then wanting. Wicked men must have had even a greater skill in leading the good astray than they have now, for they lived much longer. That wickedness abounded is beyond dispute, for Enoch died only about eighty years before Noah was born. We read that in the days of Noah, "All flesh had corrupted his way upon the earth."—Gen. 6:12. But general corruption comes on gradually. There must have been, then, great wickedness in the days of Enoch. But in the midst of it, "Enoch walked with God."—Gen. 5:22. In this simple statement is a world of meaning. It is testimony that cannot be questioned, to his complete deliverance from every sin, and to his enjoyment of every grace which is necessary to constitute a holy character. And his daily course of life was steady and uniform. He was not at one time governed by high religious principle, and at another led by Folly in her train. He exemplified holiness in all the relations of life. He was acquainted with all the cares and trials that press upon the head of a family, but his patience, his faith, his courage never gave out. As years passed over him he did not compromise as so many do, but he held out true to God to the end. He did not hold his peace in the presence of sin ; but bore an outspoken testimony against the increasing ungodliness around. Enoch prophesied, saying, "Behold, the Lord cometh with ten thousand of his saints, to execute judgment upon all, and to convince all that are ungodly among them of all their ungodly deeds which they have ungodly committed, and of all their hard speeches which ungodly sinners have spoken against him."—Jude 14, 15. This remarkable passage shows both the wickedness of the times, and the fidelity of Enoch in giving a faithful warning. It also shows that the immortality of the soul was a doctrine well understood in those days. The language plainly implies that the saints spoken of were with God, for they were to come with Him—He was not to go to them first and raise them from the grave.

During three hundred years—a period three times that of our national existence—this holy man *"walked with God."* So complete was his deliverance from sin, that even his body formed an exception and did not return to the dust. In Genesis it is said, "He was not; for God took him."—Gen. 5:24. St. Paul explains this as follows: "By faith Enoch was translated that he should not see death; and was not found, because God had translated him: for before his translation he had this testimony, that he pleased God."

NOAH. God does not leave Himself without a witness. When all flesh had corrupted his way upon the earth, and the earth was filled with

EXAMPLES OF HOLINESS

violence, Noah remained true to God. He stood alone. Wickedness was general. It was also most intense. Men lived long, and became proficients in crime. "And God saw that the wickedness of man was great in the earth, and that every imagination of the thoughts of his heart was only evil continually."—Gen. 6:5. It is impossible to describe sin as more intense, or more deeply seated. In the midst of this moral corruption, Noah lived a holy life for six hundred years. He had all the elements of true holiness.

There was a strong power of resistance. There is never an Eden on earth into which the tempter does not enter. You cannot build walls so high that they will keep out the emissaries of evil. Every apostle of truth will find it to his apparent advantage to sell out his Master. He who is willing to follow in the evil paths will never be at a loss for some to lead the way. In the most favored localities, bad examples can be found. He who takes the broad road that leadeth to destruction, will never lack for companions.

Noah's friends and neighbors, relatives and acquaintances, all forsook the service of God. In most places, here and there one can be found who has the fear of God before his eyes. But it was not so in that age of the world. Go as far as he might, in whatever direction he might, he could find no assembly of the saints—for there were no saints to assemble. Every gathering was a wicked gathering. Every man was a wicked man. To stem this current of corruption required moral energy. He had it. We may have it. The force of gravity is just as great now as it was when the world was first swung out upon its orbit. So grace does not degenerate. It can do for us all it did for the patriarchs of the infant world.

Noah was a just man. He met all his obligations, both to God and his fellow man. Some men who call themselves honest will, when opportunity offers, take advantage of those who have taken advantage of them. They try to be even with the dishonest. If the government steals from them they do not hesitate to defraud the government. If they suspect others of misrepresenting, their own representations must be taken with allowance. But Noah was just. Honesty is essential to holiness. It is but a small part of holiness, but it is a necessary part. No excess in other directions can compensate for a lack here.

He was a devout man. While walking uprightly among his fellow men he maintained a spirit of true devotion to God. In every thing he was led by the Spirit. His life was one of communion with God. His prayers and praises were not formal. He walked with God.

Without a spirit of devotion the most rigid

morality makes one but a Stoic. He is not a Christian. An essential ingredient is wanting. Without the love of God there can be no true service of God. But if we love God we shall walk with him. We shall have a consciousness of his presence. He will talk with us and we shall talk with Him.

He was consistent. His piety was all of a pattern. There was no redundancy and no lack. Some who are very devout abroad, are ill-tempered at home. Some will give liberally, but they make their money by questionable practices. Others are full of integrity, kind, polite, firm, but they encourage pride, both by silence and by example. Many hold out well for a time, and then gradually cool down to the temperature around them. But Noah was perfect in his generations. (Gen. 6:9.) He began well and he held out as he began.

In true holiness there is symmetry of character. Every one has his natural defects, but grace is intended to supply these defects. Whatever is too prominent it depresses; whatever is wrong it removes, and it furnishes whatever is lacking. Any one may become a saint. Whatever is needful for the purpose God can, by the mighty operation of His Spirit, impart. The Bible not only affirms that Noah was perfect, but the Saviour commands us to be perfect. "Be ye therefore perfect, even as your Father which is in Heaven is perfect."—Matt. 5:48. This has respect, not to any one good quality in particular, but to all good qualities. It is the practical application, made by the Saviour, of His own blessed teachings. It requires right feelings towards our fellow-men, and a course of conduct corresponding in every particular to that feeling. It enjoins love to our enemies, the kind treatment of all, and the full discharge of all the obligations which we owe to our Heavenly Father.

The end aimed at in all the teachings of the Bible, is this completeness of Christian character. "All Scripture is given by inspiration of God, and is profitable for doctrine, for reproof, for correction, for instruction in righteousness, that the man of God may be perfect, thoroughly furnished unto all good works."—II Tim. 3:16, 17.

St. Paul also tells us that it was to secure this perfection of Christian graces that the ministry was given. "And he gave some, apostles; and some, prophets; and some, evangelists; and some, pastors and teachers; for the perfecting of the saints, for the work of the ministry, for the edifying of the body of Christ: till we all come in the unity of the faith, and of the knowledge of the Son of God, unto a perfect man, unto the measure of the stature of the fulness of Christ." —Eph. 4:11-13. With all these helps, it is expected that the weakest Christian excel the mightiest saint who lived and died without these aids. "Verily I say unto you, Among them that are born of women, there hath not risen a greater than John the Baptist; notwithstanding, he that is least in the kingdom of heaven is greater than he."—Matt. 11:11. Does not the prophet refer to this when he says, "He that is feeble among them at that day shall be as David.—Zech. 12:8.

JOB. The place which the book of Job occupies in the Bible, is calculated to leave a wrong impression as to the time when he lived. We naturally suppose that the Books which are placed first were written first. But this is not always the case. Dr. George Smith in his "Patriarchal Age," shows conclusively that Job was born about two hundred and eighty years after the death of Noah. He lived in Arabia when Babylon and Assyria were in their infancy. The book of Job, probably written by Job himself, is, without doubt the oldest book in existence. As a literary production it challenges our highest admiration. Its poetry is in the most exalted strain, and its allusions to natural science have stood the test of the criticism of ages.

As to the character of Job, God himself bears the clearest testimony. He calls him his servant, and says, "There is none like him in the earth, a perfect and an upright man, one that feareth God, and escheweth evil."—Job 1:8. He manifested his piety under a great variety of circumstances, and with the most satisfactory results.

He is mentioned in the Bible as one of the three holy men who had the greatest power with God. "Though these three men, Noah, Daniel, and Job, were in it, they should deliver but their own souls by their righteousness, saith the Lord God."—Ezek. 14:14.

Let us look, first, at some of the elements of the character of this man who stood thus high in the favor of God.

He was a perfect man. The word "perfect" as used in the Bible in this, and in similar connections, is a qualifying term, not so much of degree, as of kind. It signifies "whole," "complete," with nothing lacking. It implies not an excess of one moral quality, and a corresponding lack in others, but the harmonious blending of all moral virtues in their proper proportions. There are, and always have been, but few such saints in the world. With the most, there is a want of symmetry. Their lives present the appearance of a mountainous country—sometimes up, sometimes down. Their graces are out of proportion. But Job's character was duly balanced. This is not only implied in the term "perfect," but it also appears from the other qualities ascribed to him.

He was an upright man. This is the character that man possessed before the fall. God made man upright. Job had regained this original character. He was governed in all the relations of life by the principles of sterling integrity. No opportunity to promote his personal interests could cause him to swerve from the right, in the slightest degree. The holiness that does not make men honest, is hypocrisy and not holiness.

Uprightness is that disposition which leads one to give to all that which is their due. A man who binds himself by oaths and obligations to screen from justice those with whom he is associated, cannot possibly be an upright man. The heavy oaths that are upon him make him lean from the right. As long as he acknowledges the binding force of these obligations, it is impossible for him to be an upright man. They are intended to make him lean. Unless this object is secured they are an utter failure. But Job was free to deal justly with all men. He gave no preferences to one above another on account of any associations or connections.

He feared God. He was not a cold, heathen moralist. He had a deep, abiding reverence for His Creator. The fear of incurring the displeasure of God was a controlling element in his nature. "My foot hath held his steps, his way have I kept, and not declined. Neither have I gone back from the commandment of his lips; I have esteemed the words of his mouth more than my necessary food. But he is in one mind, and who can turn him? and what his soul desireth, even that he doeth. For he performeth the thing that is appointed for me; and many such things are with him. Therefore am I troubled at his presence: when I consider, I am afraid of him."—Job 23:11–15.

There can be no true holiness without the fear of God. The piety that leaves this out, is weak and enervated, and always gives way under pressure of temptation. It is earthly in its origin, earthly in its motives, policy and tendency.

He avoided sin. This follows as a natural consequence of fearing God. "The fear of the Lord is to depart from evil." That is—it leads men to depart from all moral evil; or sin. Where wickedness openly and generally prevails, it will be found that the fear of God has been thrown off. In revivals, where the converts remain proud and dressy as before, and hold on to all their worldly associations, it will be found that the preaching is of that nature that is not calculated to produce much of the fear of God. Knowing the terrors of the Lord we persuade men. The old revivalists, such as Wesley, Edwards, Knapp and Redfield, whose converts generally held out in the narrow way, were men who proclaimed the law of God in thunder tones, and laid the foundation for a genuine Christian experience and a consistent

Christian life, by begetting in the minds of their hearers a salutary fear of God.

Job exemplified the principles of holiness in all the relations of life, and under the most trying circumstances.

As a father, how careful he was of the spiritual welfare of his children! "And it was so when the days of their feasting were gone about, that Job sent and sanctified them, and rose up early in the morning, and offered burnt-offering according to the number of them all: for Job said, It may be that my sons have sinned, and cursed God in their hearts. Thus did Job continually."—Job 1:5.

As a ruler—for Job as a patriarch was a ruler among his people,—he was just and merciful. Such was his uprightness as a judge that he was treated with the greatest respect by all. "When I went out to the gate through the city, when I prepared my seat in the street!"—where to this day in oriental cities judges hold their courts,— "The young men saw me and hid themselves: and the aged arose, and stood up. The princes refrained talking, and laid their hand on their mouth. The nobles held their peace, and their tongue cleaved to the roof of their mouth. When the ear heard me, then it blessed me; and when the eye saw me, it gave witness to me: because I delivered the poor that cried, and the fatherless, and him that had none to help him. The blessing of him that was ready to perish came upon me: and I caused the widow's heart to sing for joy. I put on righteousness, and it clothed me: my judgment was as a robe and a diadem. I was eyes to the blind, and feet was I to the lame. I was a father to the poor: and the cause which I knew not I searched out. And I brake the jaws of the wicked, and plucked the spoil out of his teeth."—Job. 29:7-17.

Would that all our magistrates were men of this character. Thus did Job exemplify holiness in prosperity.

But reverses came upon him. His children were cut down suddenly by the whirlwind's stroke. His property was swept away; a foul disease preyed upon his body; his friends decided against him—as friends are very apt to do when we need them most; and even the wife of his bosom turned against him, and reproachingly said, "Dost thou still retain thine integrity? curse God, and die."—Job 2:9. Yet under this accumulation of trials, Job's faith in God never for an instant gave way. He maintained his fidelity to God to the last.

True holiness is adapted to us equally in all the relations and in all the circumstances of life. It is a crown of beauty to the young, an unfailing source of strength to the middle-aged, an unwavering support to the aged, and to all a safe covering from the scorching rays of prosperity and the blasting storms of adversity. Follow holiness without which no man shall see the Lord.

CHAPTER XVII.

LIMITS OF SANCTIFICATION.

HOLINESS is popular. There is great danger of its being carried too far. Already the effort is being made to sanctify things that cannot be sanctified.

There is a limit to the subjects of sanctification. There are some things which, from their nature, are not capable of being made holy. The best mathematician cannot teach an ox the multiplication table, or teach a horse algebra. A church raised up in the providence of God to spread Scriptural holiness through the land, cannot make gambling holy, or sanctify pride. The things which God forbids, should be put away and not reformed. All attempts at reforming things forbidden by the word of God, should be abandoned. God lays the axe at the root of the tree. Let us ply our blows there, and though the tree may seem as flourishing as ever, yet work on and it will fall when the roots are severed. You may trim at the branches and show results in the handful of severed twigs you bear off in triumph, but the tree will only be the more vigorous from the pruning.

Money-worship cannot be sanctified. In the eyes of the world men are estimated less by their worth than by their wealth. The ability to gain and hold wealth is treated as a cardinal virtue. Bad, incompetent men are elected and appointed to high official positions, for no other reason than because they are rich. This mammon worship is wrong. It is idolatry. It is degrading to manhood and insulting to God. It is wholly bad— bad in itself. It cannot be sanctified by taking it into the house of God and making it contribute to the support of the Gospel. It is as wrong to give a man a seat in the house of God *because* he is rich, as it is to give him a seat in Congress, or in the Cabinet, for the same reason. It is as wicked to trade in pews as it is to trade in votes. It is just as corrupt to buy one's way to a front seat in a church, as it is to buy a seat in the Legislature. The principle that lies at the bottom is, a servile acknowledgement of the Almighty Dollar. It is giving money preference over the man. It is placing a lower estimate upon Christian virtues than upon money. It is paying the homage to gold that is due only to merit. This principle cannot be sanctified. It should be put away from the house of God entirely. Men should stand there, as men. There should no preference be given to one over another on account of wealth. The rich and the poor should meet together, feeling that the Lord is the Maker of us all.

Pride cannot be sanctified. It may be introduced into holy places, but such an introduction does not make it holy. A jewel may be inserted in the flesh—heathens hang them in the nose—Christians in the ears—but it does not become flesh. It may produce inflammation, but it cannot add to the strength. Pride may enter largely into the construction and furnishing of edifices consecrated to sacred uses, but this does not render the pride sacred. God speaks of those who anciently introduced unauthorized refinements into His worship, as "A people that provoketh me to anger continually to my face; that sacrificeth in gardens, and burneth incense upon altars of brick."—Isa. 65:3. To display pride and fashion—badges of the love of the world—in the church, is as if the wife should present herself to her husband adorned with the rings and jewels of his wicked rival and enemy. "Ye adulterers and adulteresses, know ye not that the friendship of the world is enmity with God? Whosoever, therefore, will be a friend of the world is the enemy of God."—Jas. 4:4.

The attempt to sanctify the drama, by making sabbath school children actors, the church the theatre, and preachers and leaders the managers, can only result in dragging the actors down, in-

LIMITS OF SANCTIFICATION. 115

stead of elevating the stage. Priests and monks tried the same experiment hundreds of years ago, taking their characters from the Bible, and their spirit from the world, until they made Christianity contemptible, by sinking its votaries to the level of the heathen, in morality.

The effort to sanctify things which should have been put away, has been a prolific cause of the corruption of the church in all ages. After the conversion of Constantine, the Bishops in their zeal for the conversion of the heathen, adopted the heathen rites and called them by Christian names; just as the Churches now, to draw in the world, adopt worldly pleasures and attempt to throw over them a religious garb. Mosheim says, "The rites and institutions, by which the Greeks, Romans, and other nations, had formerly testified their religious veneration for fictitious deities, were now adopted, with some slight alterations, by Christian bishops, and employed in the service of the true God. These fervent heralds of the Gospel, whose zeal outran their candor and integrity, imagined that the nations would receive Christianity with more facility, when they saw the rites and ceremonies to which they were accustomed, adopted in the church, and the same worship paid to Christ and His martyrs, which they had formerly offered to their idol deities. Hence it happened, that, in these times, the religion of the

Greeks and Romans differed very little, in its external appearance, from that of the Christians. They had both a most pompous and splendid ritual. Gorgeous robes, mitres, tiaras, wax-tapers, crosiers, processions, lustrations, images, gold and silver vases, and many such circumstances of pageantry, were equally to be seen in the heathen temples and in the Christian churches." From the fiercest persecutions the church of Jesus Christ rapidly recovered and came out purer and stronger from the fiery ordeal. But from the attempt to sanctify heathen rites and heathen temples the church has never recovered. The most numerous and the most powerful of all the churches that bear the Christian name, the Roman Catholic, has to-day more of the spirit and practice of the old pagan churches than of the church founded by Jesus Christ.

CHAPTER XVIII.

A PRESENT EXPERIENCE.

THE salvation of the Gospel is present as well as prospective. To one who had always lived under ground, and never seen the sun, the promise of enjoying the sunshine in years to come would have but little meaning. His only idea of the splendor of the sun would be such as he could gather from multiplying the rays of his mining lamps. But we, who live above-ground, and enjoy the light and heat of the sun, expect to see it to-morrow, because we see it to-day. So we expect to be saved eternally, because we are saved in time. "Behold now is the day of salvation." It was a devout Calvinist who wrote,

"The grace that saves the soul from hell,
  Will save from present sin."

The idea runs all through the Gospel that salvation is a present reality. It is something that is experienced and enjoyed from day to day. Jesus says, "Now ye are clean through the word which I have spoken unto you." He does not say, "shall be," as though the day of deliverance was in the future. And Paul writes, "By grace are ye saved, through faith." Thus the salvation provided in Christ is every where spoken of as something which has a positive existence in the heart of every believer.

It is a great mistake, which many professing Christians make, that of throwing their salvation into the future. Ask them, if they are saved, and the answer is, "I hope I shall be." What is the ground of this hope? The assent of the mind to the truth, and perhaps membership in an orthodox Church. But "the devils believe and tremble." Yet they are devils still. It is a great blessing to be able to see the truth, and to have the courage to stand by it. But unless you go farther than to join the church even, and attend its ordinances, you can never be saved. Judas went to perdition from the bosom of the Master and the company of the Apostles. The road to hell is just as direct from the Church as it is from the world. What you need, in order that you may be saved in Heaven at last, is, to be saved *now*, from the guilt and from the power of sin, and to keep saved unto the end.

If you are in a state of salvation, you know it. You cannot have victory over impatience, over the world, over the trials of daily life, and be ignorant of the fact. If your appetites master your reason, and your conscience, you can but be aware, to some extent at least, that you are under bondage. So, when deliverance comes, you can but realize the greatness of the change. If, instead of a spirit of murmuring and fretfulness, the peace of God that passeth all understanding reigns in your heart, you must be conscious of it yourself, and it must be obvious to all around you. Then do not yield to the delusion, that, if you believe you are saved you will be saved. Take up with nothing short of present deliverance from pride and impatience, and all sinful inclinations and sinful desires. Recall the convictions you have had in other days. God has not changed. The self-denials, the separation from the world that He then required, He still requires. The cross that stood in your way then, stands in your way now. You have not gone around it. You have gone back. You must take it up before you can make any further progress. You do not feel as much disturbed now, as you did then, because your conscience is becoming seared. The peace which you profess to feel is delusive. It is insensibility, and not peace. You are in danger of becoming "past feeling." Welcome conviction. Take up the cross that lies before you. If it is laying aside ornamental attire, let it go at once. You can carry no garment' beyond the grave, but the robe washed white in Jesus' blood. If you have taken a wrong position, in regard to the work of God, denouncing as fanaticism the operations of the Spirit, hesitate not to confess it. If you have wronged others, make all the confession and the restitution that the circumstances demand. Not only your usefulness, but your soul is at stake. "If we walk in the light as he is in the light, we have fellowship one with another, and the blood of Jesus Christ his Son cleanseth us from all sin."—I John 1:7. Resolve to be right.

CHAPTER XIX.

HOW OBTAINED.

WE use the word sanctified in this chapter, in its fullest sense, as equivalent to sanctified wholly.

Determination is the first great essential to being sanctified to God. No matter how deeply ones feelings may be wrought upon, he will not go through, unless he is fully decided to be holy, and to lead a holy life.

This decision must be an independent one. It will not do to have any secret reservation. Many profess holiness as long as they have a preacher that preaches holiness. Then, if they get another pastor, who preaches *publicly* in a Christian pulpit, but worships *secretly* at the altars of Baal, or the shrine of fashion, they will follow their preacher wherever he leads. No one, while thus undecided, can ever obtain true holiness. There must be the decision of Joshua. "But as for me and my house, we will serve the Lord."—Josh. 24:15. Others may make an opposite choice; I may grieve over the wrong choice they make, but I will not be governed by it. If the multitude goes right, I will rejoice in it; but if they go wrong, I will not go with them. It is not in battalions that we march up the path of life: it is in single file that we press along the narrow way. It is for want of this independent determination that so many who profess holiness do not hold out. They lean on others, and when their earthly supports give way they fall back into the crowded ranks of worldlings in a semi-Christian guise.

This decision must be self-sacrificing. He who will be holy while it is popular, or profitable, will never become holy at all. The very essence of holiness is the extinction of selfishness. It requires just as much of the martyr spirit to be a holy man or woman to-day, as it did in the days when they exposed holy men and women to be torn in pieces by wild beasts, or chained them to the stake to be burned. The spirit of persecution is not dead. The old antagonism between sin and holiness still remains. Christ and Belial sustain no more friendly relations to each other than they did in the days of the apostle. It is still true that "Whosoever will be a friend of the world is the enemy of God."—Jas. 4:4. There must be a willingness to encounter its hostility, to endure the worst that it can inflict upon us. In the 14th chapter of St. Luke are recorded several illustrations which our Lord uses to show the necessity of counting the cost, by all who would be His disciples. "So likewise, whosoever he be of you that forsaketh not all that he hath, he cannot be my disciple."

If, then, you would obtain true holiness, you must count it of more value, not only than any *one* thing; but more than *all* things else. Things that were the greatest sources of joy to you must be abandoned if they stand in the way of living a holy life.

To obtain holiness we must sanctify ourselves. This is the Lord's order as laid down in both the Old and the New Testament. He who prays for a harvest, must, if he would not mock God, prepare his ground, and sow, and till, and guard against destructive forces, in a proper manner. So he who would be holy, must break up the fallow ground of his heart, and sow to himself in righteousness. To secure spiritual results, it is just as necessary to meet the conditions which God has established, as it is to meet physical conditions to secure desired material results. The laws of the spiritual kingdom are as inflexible as those of the vegetable kingdom. No amount of faith, or of praying, can take the place of the work which God requires us to do. We must show our faith by our works.

See how explicit are the directions which God gives to those who would be holy. "For I am the Lord your God: ye shall therefore sanctify yourselves, and ye shall be holy."—Lev. 11:44.

"Sanctify yourselves, therefore, and be ye holy: for I am the Lord your God."—Lev. 20:7. "And let the priests also, which come near to the Lord, sanctify themselves, lest the Lord break forth upon them."—Ex. 19:52. These passages teach that we must separate ourselves from every thing that is impure; and set ourselves apart for holy purposes, and God will make us holy. But our part of the work must be done first. All that is necessary for God to do to enable us to do our part, he does in advance. God works in us to will and to do, but he can go no farther towards making us saints, unless we work out our own salvation as He works within us, by His blessed Spirit. We are to go to the extent of our ability before we have any right to expect supernatural aid. Holiness is a voluntary state. A man is not a machine. His freedom of will alone renders him capable of holiness. The New Testament teaching is to the same effect.

"Having therefore these promises, dearly beloved, let us cleanse ourselves from all filthiness of the flesh and spirit, perfecting holiness in the fear of God."—II Cor. 7:1. Here is taught the second blessing. They are "dearly beloved;" that is, real Christians. They already were holy in part. "Perfecting holiness" implies that the work of holiness was already begun in them. Especially notice the part enjoined upon us in this passage. We are to "cleanse ourselves."

We must not ask the Lord to do what we can do. If tobacco is not a "filthiness of the flesh" we are at a loss to know what can possibly come under that head. If you use it, you can throw it away; you can wash your mouth; then you are prepared to pray in faith for God to deliver you from the appetite. He has done it for thousands —He can do it for you. Pride is a filthiness of the spirit. God treats it as such. It is so offensive that He does not come near it, "But the proud he knoweth afar off."—Ps. 138:6. We can lay aside all its outward manifestations, and then, with confidence ask God to take the unholy disposition from our hearts.

Again the apostle says, "I beseech you therefore, brethren, by the mercies of God, that ye present your bodies a living sacrifice, holy, acceptable unto God, which is your reasonable service."—Rom. 12:1. Here again, we have the second blessing. They were already *brethren*. But in order to *prove* that "this is the will of God, even your sanctification," we are entreated to "present our bodies *a living sacrifice*."

This implies a consecration of every thing, even our lives, to the service of God. All our powers are to be employed as He directs. If our bodies are given to God, they must be fed and clothed and used for Him. We cannot follow the fashions of the world in any particular in which they conflict with the plain directions that God has given. We must be directed by God in our business, and in all the affairs of life.

To obtain entire sanctification we must confess our inbred sins, our sinful dispositions, which to a greater or less extent remain after one is truly sanctified to God. "If we confess our sins, he is faithful and just to forgive us our sins, and to cleanse us from all unrighteousness." —1 Jno. 1:9. That is, if we confess the sins we have committed, God is faithful to forgive us; for He has promised to do it. If we confess our inbred sins He is faithful to cleanse us from them—*from all unrighteousness*. This is what Mr. Wesley means by the "Repentance of believers." "The repentance consequent upon justification, is widely different from that which is antecedent to it. This implies no guilt, no sense of condemnation, no consciousness of the wrath of God. It does not suppose any doubt of the favor of God or any 'fear that hath torment.' It is properly a conviction, wrought by the Holy Ghost, of the *sin* which still *remains* in our heart; of the Φρονημα σαρκος, *the carnal mind* which does still remain (as our church speaks) even in them that are regenerate; although it does no longer reign; it has not now dominion over them. It is a conviction of our proneness to evil, of a heart bent to backsliding, of the still continuing tendency of the flesh to lust against the Spirit. Sometimes, unless we continually watch and pray, it lusteth to pride, sometimes to anger, sometimes to love of the world, love of ease, love of honor or love of pleasure more than of God. It is a conviction of the tendency of our heart to self-will, to atheism or idolatry, and, above all, to unbelief, whereby, in a thousand ways, and under a thousand pretences, we are ever departing, more or less, from the living God."

To be sanctified wholly we must trust implicitly in God, through the merits of Jesus Christ to do the work now. Just as long as we put it off in the future, just so long the work will be delayed. A belief that it will be done sometime will not bring the blessing. Nor will the faith that saves spring up of itself, if we meet all the other conditions. It is an active trust that must be voluntarily, consciously exercised. "But what is the faith whereby we are sanctified, saved from sin and perfected in love? It is a divine evidence and conviction, first, that God hath promised it in the Holy Scripture. Secondly. It is a divine evidence and conviction, that what God hath promised He is able to perform. It is, thirdly, a divine evidence and conviction that He is able and willing to do it now. And why not? Is not a moment to Him the same as a thousand years? He cannot want more time to accomplish whatever is His will."

Again: "Certainly you may look for it now, if you believe it is by faith, and by this token you may surely know whether you seek it by faith or by works. If by works, you want something to be done first, before you are sanctified. You think, I must first be or do thus or thus. Then you are seeking it by works unto this day. If you seek it by faith, you may expect it as you are; and if as you are, then expect it now."

CHAPTER XX.

HOW RETAINED.

IT is not necessary to teach us how to lose our health. Works on Hygiene do not attempt to do that. A simple neglect of the laws of health will bring on disorder, disease, and finally death. To become a confirmed dyspeptic one does not need to commit some striking and wilful act of disobedience to the laws of our physical being. Many a person has lost his health without being able to tell how he lost it.

So the Bible does not teach us how to lose holiness. It gives us very explicit directions how to keep it. We give a few. "The Lord make you to increase and abound in love one toward another, and toward all men even as we do toward you: to the end he may stablish your hearts unblameable in holiness before God, even our Father, at the coming of our Lord Jesus Christ with all his saints."—I Thess. 3:12, 13. "If ye do these things ye shall never fall, for so an entrance shall be ministered unto you abundantly into the everlasting kingdom of our Lord and Saviour Jesus Christ."—II Peter 1:10, 11. "Who are kept by the power of God through faith unto salvation ready to be revealed in the last times."—I Peter 1:5. Notice, in each of these passages there is something spoken of for us to do if we would keep holiness and get through to Heaven. In the first, we are told that we must "increase and abound in love one toward another and toward all men." What we had when we were converted, or when we were sanctified wholly is not sufficient. It is not enough that we grow in knowledge; there must be a marked increase in love. We must abound in it—not merely toward those who love us, but toward "all men."

In the second passage we are directed to do certain things. By reference to the preceding verses we shall find that the "things to be done" in order that we may "never fall," are Christian graces to be added to the beginnings of these graces received when we were converted and when we were sanctified wholly.

Some lakes and inland seas are without outlets; but none are without inlets. Insensible evaporation would soon dry up the largest of them, if its waters were not receiving a constant addition. The sturdiest tree would soon die if it could derive no nourishment from earth or air. So, no matter how much grace a person received when he was converted, and how great an increase was realized when he was sanctified wholly, if he does not go on in his experience and grow in grace he will become dry and unfruitful, spiritually dead, and insensible to his condition. His outward conduct may be without reproach, but his power is gone. To keep a house in good order repairs must be made as need requires; to keep wealth one must be acquiring wealth; to keep learning one must be adding to his store of learning, and to keep holiness one must be steadily "perfecting holiness in the fear of the Lord."

In the third passage quoted, we are taught that it is the power of God that keeps us. This is frequently stated in the Scriptures. "Now unto him that is able to keep you from falling, and to present you faultless before the presence of his glory with exceeding joy."—Jude 24. God's power is adequate to carry us safely through any emergency that can possibly arise. However numerous and strong may be our enemies, God can easily overcome them. Whatever difficulties may stand in our way He can remove them. If a sea lies in our path He can open a passage through it. If a mountain would stop our progress He can give us wings like an eagle and enable us to soar above it. In the furnace He can keep us. In the desert He can feed us. Nothing is too great or too hard for the power of God. It is almighty. He who is kept by the power of God is kept in safety. He is willing, nay anxious to keep us all. He is just as ready to keep one as another. Then why are not all kept? The reason is found in us, and not in God. We are kept through faith. This faith is a voluntary trust on our part. One is kept, because he, of his own free will, exercises faith in God. Another doubts, and thus severs his union with God, and he in consequence falls into darkness and at last into sin.

There are many passages of Scripture which teach that we are kept by the infinite love and power of God. But, like those we have considered, they imply or express conditions which we are to meet. These conditions are important. If we meet them, we keep the grace which God has given us. If we fail to meet them then we lose the blessing of holiness. Many lose it in this way without knowing it. This was the case with the minister of the church of Ephesus. He was so active, so patient, so orthodox, and so zealous for the purity of the church that he had not the slightest idea that he had met with any serious loss. His zeal against evil-doers and false teachers, had taken the place of the tender love he had in other days. He considered himself radical, and uncompromising, and estabished in the faith. But Christ pronounced him fallen.

Reader, have you had a clear experience of being sanctified wholly? If not, then seek it at once. You cannot afford to live another day without it.

If you have obtained this blessing are you keeping it. clear and fresh? You may keep up the profession. Many do, long after they have lost the blessing. There may be nothing particularly amiss in their conduct or conversation, but they do not bring forth the fruits of holiness. They have not its joy or its power. They lack its gentleness, its meekness, its simplicity. Their profession is based upon reasoning or habit, and not upon the direct witness of the Spirit.

Beloved, how is it with you at the present time? Are you fulfilling the conditions on which the keeping of the blessing of holiness depends? If you are not increasing and abounding in that tender, unselfish love that makes you careful of the reputation of others, and considerate of their interests and happiness; if you are reckless in your statements, and ready with damaging insinuations against those who do not agree with your opinions; or if, on the other hand, you are light and trifling, gradually conforming to the world in your conversation, in your dress, and in your business, then you have every reason to believe that you have lost the blessing of holiness. Be honest with yourself: welcome the light, and humble yourself before God, and seek to be right with Him no matter how much of humiliation it may involve.

CHAPTER XXI.

HOW LOST.

HOLINESS is voluntary. It is a moral state. But a moral action implies freedom of choice. No one is praised or blamed, rewarded or punished, for doing that which could not possibly be avoided. But the holy are rewarded, the unholy are punished. Therefore a holy person is holy from choice.

But a voluntary state may be lost. The helm that can be turned in a right direction can also be turned in a wrong direction. The vessel that has been kept in the channel for years may at last, be run upon a rock.

One who has walked in the way of holiness for a season, may yield to temptation and turn aside. It is true that the longer one walks with God, the more securely he walks. The nearer a body moves to the sun, the stronger it is attracted towards the sun. But comets that come very near to the sun at times, finally take a turn and fly off into space. Those who get very near to the Lord are likely to press on and grow in grace; but they may fall, and get away from the Lord.

David was, for years, a holy man, fully approved of the Lord; but he fell into sin. Paul was caught up into the third heaven where he saw things that language could not describe. Yet Paul was keenly alive to the fact that he might lose the grace he had received and be finally lost. His watchfulness was great and constant. He says, "I keep under my body and bring it into subjection: lest that by any means, when I have preached to others, I myself should be a castaway."—I Cor. 9:27. It is evident then, that one who has experienced the blessing of holiness, can lose it. He need not; he should not—but still he may. There is a possibility that he may fall away.

In what relation does one stand to God who has lost the blessing of holiness? Can one lose the blessing of entire sanctification and still retain the blessing of justification? These are important questions which should be examined carefully.

When one falls into actual sin he loses both justification and sanctification. He falls into condemnation. He is no longer a saint; he becomes a sinner. If he gets back to God, he must come confessing his sins and seeking pardon. "Brethren, if any of you do err from the truth, and one convert him; let him know, that he which converteth the sinner from the error of his way shall save a soul from death, and shall hide a multitude of sins."—Jas. 5:19, 20. It is a *brother* who has erred. Not a false professor, but a real Christian. He is to be converted like any other sinner. If not converted, his soul is in danger of death.

Again one may lose the blessing of entire sanctification by giving way to doubts and unbelief. It is by faith we stand. Whatsoever ground we gain by faith we hold by faith. By unbelief we lose it. He who walks on the water by faith, goes down, as fear supplants his faith. One may also lose the blessing of holiness by failing to confess it. In the same degree that profession becomes indefinite, the experience becomes indefinite. Doubt lies at the bottom of this want of confession. Satan is ever ready to accuse a saint of God. But to hold his ground he must keep fully consecrated to God and confess out boldly all that God does for him. "And they overcame him by the blood of the Lamb, and by the word of their testimony: and they loved not their lives unto the death."—Rev. 12:11.

When one listens to the accusations of Satan and fails to bear a clear testimony of his being washed by the blood of the Lamb, he loses the blessing. The witness is gone. But he does not necessarily fall into sin. He may still be keenly alive to the fear of God. He may still watch against sin and have victory over it. He may still truly love God and faithfully endeavor to keep all His commandments. Such a person in losing the blessing of holiness has not lost his justification. He is still a child of God. He is sensible of what he has lost and strives to regain it.

To do this it is not necessary that he should throw up all profession of religion and begin anew. He is not unholy; but he is holy only in part. He should pray to be sanctified wholly. He should confess what he has lost. He should consecrate up to all the light that God has given him. He should exercise faith in the atoning blood to be again cleansed from all sin. He should make no delay, nor wait for some great crisis to occur—but should at once come to God to be saved to the uttermost.

Mr. Fletcher lost the blessing of holiness three times in immediate succession, by a simple failure to confess it. But he did not rest until he sought and found the grace, and was established in it.

If you lose any degree of grace, seek to gain it at once and do not wait till you have lost more till you make a vigorous effort to regain it. "Return unto me and I will return unto you, saith the Lord of hosts."—Mal. 3:7.

"Can one lose the blessing of holiness without losing his justification?"

We answer this question again.

Without *any degree* of holiness one cannot be in a state of salvation. He who is destitute of holiness is not justified. Many appear to think that they can possess saving grace without any measure of holiness. This is a fundamental error. When God forgives, he says, with power, "Go, sin no more." Such a change is wrought, instantaneously, in the moral nature of one whom God forgives, that from that moment he has power over his sinful appetites and passions. We must never lose sight of the great truth that "He that committeth sin is of the devil."— I John 3:8. In the popular religion of the day, this plain statement of the beloved disciple is completely disregarded. It is treated as though it were an interpolation, wholly inconsistent with the general teaching of the Word of God. But the whole tenor of the Scripture is in harmony with the teaching of St. John. There is not, when rightly understood, a contradictory passage in the Bible. St. Paul says, "And such were some of you; but ye are washed, but ye are sanctified, but ye are justified in the name of the Lord Jesus, and by the Spirit of our God."— I Cor. 6:11. Notice the order, washed, sanctified, justified. This is God's order in saving a soul. An unwashed sinner, wallowing in his sins, is not justified. When forgiven he is sanctified, not only in the sense of *consecrated*—that is set apart to do God's will—but in the sense of made holy. Not only has he sanctified himself, but he *is sanctified*—that is, God has sanctified him, actually made him holy. From being a sinner he has become, in an important sense, a holy man. Being thus washed, and sanctified, he is at the same time, justified,—that is forgiven—and placed in a state of acceptance with God.

But mark! It does not say sanctified wholly —entirely. He is so far sanctified that he has power over sin. He is not under the dominion of any of his former sinful appetites or habits. Sin does not have dominion over him as it once did. But he feels sinful tendencies remaining in his heart. He has, at times, to repress pride, to keep it down. He does not yield to anger, but sometimes he feels it, and suppresses it. He comes to God, confesses and bewails these inbred sins and is cleansed from them. He reads, "And the very God of peace sanctify you wholly." He believes for it to be done in himself—and it is done. He is sanctified wholly.

Can he be kept in this state? He can. "I pray God your whole spirit and soul and body be preserved blameless unto the coming of our Lord Jesus Christ."—I Thess. 5:23. But our being kept in this state depends upon our meeting certain conditions. 1. We must steadily believe. "Kept by the power of God through faith unto salvation."—I Pet. 1:5. 2. Suitable confession.

"With the mouth confession is made unto salvation."—Romans 10:10. 3. Obedience. "He became the author of eternal salvation unto all them that obey him."—Heb. 5:9.

We see then that the blessing of holiness may be lost by doubting, by failing to confess what God has done for us, and also by actual willful disobedience. When one loses the blessing of holiness by transgression, as David did, he loses all. He is no longer justified. If he ever gets back to God it must be by repentance and confession. His prayer, in substance, must be, "Have mercy upon me, O God, according to thy loving kindness, according unto the multitude of thy tender mercies blot out my transgressions. Wash me thoroughly from mine iniquity, and cleanse me from my sin."—Ps. 51:1, 2. In a case like this, when one loses holiness he loses justification. There is no controversy about this, all admit it.

But when one loses the blessing of holiness by giving way to doubts and fears, under manifold temptations, the case is different. He has not willingly given up anything. The blessing is gone. He feels it—he laments it. He cries out, "O that I knew where I might find him!"

When I was pastor of a church which held to the doctrine of holiness in theory, and persecuted those who enjoyed it, one of our members, a quiet, conscientious man, obtained the blessing of entire sanctification. He was as happy as he could be and continue in the body. He testified to the blessing, with great power. But when he attended his class meeting, and his turn came to speak, the enemy, transformed as an angel of light, suggested, "If you profess the blessing of holiness, your leader will not receive it, for he does not believe the doctrine, but if you say you are very happy you will confess the truth and no opposition will be aroused." He followed the suggestion. But he had no sooner sat down than great darkness came upon him, which lasted several months. But all this time he was one of the most careful, conscientious Christians. He had lost the blessing of holiness, but he had not lost his justification.

Then our answer to the question is, "It depends on *how* one loses the blessing of holiness whether he loses justification at the same time."

Sweeping declarations are seldom true. They need generally to be qualified. It is not best, unnecessarily, to discourage those who have lost some of the grace they once enjoyed. When they are on their backs the way to recover them is not to cut off their heads. Encourage them to hold fast that which they have, and to seek for more. Do not fall into the mistake that to be faithful, you must discredit the professions of those whose lives are in harmony with their professions, because they were not saved under your labors. God has many saints that you never saw nor helped. Satan is the accuser of the brethren. Suspicion is no proof of piety. Be more ready to build up than to tear down, to lead on than to drive back. "Comfort ye, comfort ye my people, saith your God."—Isa. 40:1.

CHAPTER XXII.

PROFESSING HOLINESS.

IT is a subtle artifice of Satan to try to get us to make the performance of *one* duty answer for the performance of another duty equally plain and important. This is a point that needs to be well guarded.

If you would be holy you must live holiness. This is of the utmost importance. But when the false teachers tell you that this can take the place of a *profession* of holiness do not listen to them.

Profess holiness, if you have holiness. No matter how unpopular it may be, confess out all that the Lord does for you. "For with the heart man believeth unto righteousness; and with the mouth confession is made unto salvation."—Rom. 10:10. Mark. It is with *the mouth* that confession is made. Keep up the confession until you reach eternal salvation.

The word "sanctify" is one of the words of Christ. It will not do to be ashamed of it. Christ prayed for His disciples, "Sanctify them through thy truth."—John 17:17. If the prayer is fully answered, you dishonor Christ by confessing that it is answered in part. That is not the way men do in business. When a request is fully met they acknowledge it fully. If Christ not only forgives you, but sanctifies you, then it is not enough to say that you are forgiven. That is not the whole truth.

An indefinite profession will lead to an indefinite experience. The eye that is not used grows dim. The faith that is not professed, for fear of giving offence, vanishes. "From him that hath not," so surely that he cannot profess it, "shall be taken away even that which he hath."—Matt. 25:29. Profess out clearly and definitely all that God does for you. Only see to it, as an old writer says, "That the bottom of your life is on a level with the top of your profession." Let the most objectionable things that you do be perfectly consistent with the highest profession that you make.

If you enjoy it, and live it, by all means profess it. If God sets this great light in the soul no one has a right to cover it up. Let it shine. Confess all that Divine grace does for you. No one can long retain this great blessing without letting it be known that God bestows it upon him. He would have others encouraged to come to Him for the fullness of grace, and so He would have those upon whom He bestows it declare His faithfulness. "All thy works shall praise thee, O Lord; and thy saints shall bless thee. They shall speak of the glory of thy kingdom, and talk of thy power; to make known to the sons of men his mighty acts, and the glorious majesty of his kingdom."—Ps. 145:10-12. A holy heart is pre-eminently the work of the Lord. It is a creation which His power alone can effect. It is the glory of His kingdom. Nothing demands a greater exercise of Omnipotence than to make a depraved human heart holy. Wherever this mighty act has been performed, the saints of God should make it known. They should freely and explicitly confess it, to the glory of His name. But professions, of themselves, amount to nothing. Unfounded professions are common. They are probably not made, in many cases, wilfully; but in general, once had a good foundation, and are kept up from habit, and from the vain hope that the blessing is not lost, but only the witness of it. These professors are aware that their strength is gone; but they still think it best to make as strong a show of resistance as possible; as Lee kept McClellan at bay by pointing long wooden cannon toward his camp. That there are those who really enjoy the blessing of holiness we have no doubt. Precious humble souls, they are walking in all lowliness before the Lord. May your numbers be multiplied, and your graces be strengthened and increased!

There are others whose professions are not well founded. This is evident from their fruits. A good tree cannot bring forth evil fruit.

Some are wanting in temperance. Their appetites have the ascendency over them. They do not keep their bodies under. Deprive them of their tobacco for a single day and they are miserable. It does not seem to me that we have a right to profess holiness if the deprivation, in the providence of God, of any particular thing to eat or drink makes us wretched. If the Lord gives us enough to keep soul and body together, we should accept it with thankfulness, and go on our way rejoicing. Temperance—in the original ἐγκράτεια—signifies self control, having the mastery over one's appetites, and if you have not this mastery, do not profess holiness until you obtain it. God can give it to you. Seek it earnestly. It may cost you a conflict, but the victory will be worth resistance even unto blood.

Some are wanting in self-denial. They profess to have renounced themselves—their own righteousness and ease, and interests, and yet they seem to forget that this renunciation amounts to nothing, unless it embraces particulars. It would puzzle them to tell wherein they deny themselves of any coveted gratification for Christ's sake. We heard recently of some precious saints in affluent circumstances, who, after giving all they could for the relief of the starving Lancashire sufferers, deprived themselves of the use of butter, that they might have more to give. In some form or other, self-denial must be practised daily if the blessing of holiness would be retained.

Some are wanting in non-conformity to the world. Satan has convinced them, and alas! they were but too easily convinced, that to gain an influence over worldly, gay professors, and lead them into the blessing of holiness, they must not be too strict, but must conform to worldly fashions to a degree that the Spirit of God would not allow, if they listened to His dictates. O, what a fearful mistake is this! To have God receive us we must come out *and be separate.* There is but one mediator between God and man, and none, that we read of, between the church and the world; and he who assumes to occupy that dubious position will, at the last day, notwithstanding all the wonderful works that he has done, hear Christ say, "Depart from me, I know you not." The heaviest blows that have been ever inflicted upon Christianity, have been given by this class of persons. Without designing it perhaps, they have, by little and little, lowered the standard of the Gospel, until the church has become deluged with a tide of worldliness that threatens to sweep away the last vestige of spiritual life. The Church grew strong and multiplied under the cruelties of

Nero and Domitian; but from the effects of the patronage of Constantine it has never recovered unto this day.

It is distressing to hear persons professing holiness when decked out in "gold and pearls and costly array," and to hear them say with a show of great self-complacency when their inconsistency is hinted at, "O my conscience does not condemn me," just as if their conscience were a substitute for the explicit word of God.

Some are wanting in humility. They may be plain in their apparel, but there is about them an appearance of pride and self-conceit. They are forward and positive in expressing their opinions, and seem to think that nothing is done right in which they do not participate. Let us remember, beloved, that perfect love is never found only in connection with the deepest humility. Do not take up more time in meetings than belongs to you. If you are a minister, and occupy your hour in preaching, do give the people an opportunity to witness in the social meetings, and do not yourself occupy half the time. Such a course does not savor of humility. There may be others who have not the gift of utterance that you have, who have yet a much richer experience in the things of God; it would do you and others good to listen to them. If you have true humility, one effect will be to make you "swift to hear and slow to speak."

Others are wanting in love. They may be rooted and grounded in doctrine, but not in love. They cannot bear much. They are quick and sensitive. In their intercourse with their families there is what sounds and looks very much like fretfulness. Little things chafe, annoy and irritate. This cannot be where true holiness is enjoyed. It produces a calm quiet and evenness of temper that makes itself felt everywhere, and especially in the family circle. We may be firm and decided with our children without being cross. Anything like scolding will not only hurt us but hurt them. If necessary to use the rod of correction, do not spare to use it, but let it be in love.

Let us, beloved, search ourselves. We may be right. Whatever our trials, God is willing and desirous to give all needed grace. "Hold fast the profession of your faith without wavering," and then live up to your profession.

It is of no use to profess holiness unless you enjoy it in your life. That you had it once, is no evidence that you have it now. You may still be orthodox in your doctrines, strictly moral in your life, faithful in the performance of all the common, outward duties of religion,—nay, you may even be devoted to the advocacy of holiness, without truly possessing this grace. "Were a man," says Wesley, "as harmless as a post, he might be as far from holiness as heaven from earth." Holiness is our complete renewal in the image of God,—the perfect love of God shed abroad in the heart by the Holy Ghost given unto us, so that we love God with all our heart, and mind, and strength, and our neighbor as ourself.

It is not merely victory over sin,—this is given to every pardoned soul,—but it is deliverance from sinful tempers themselves. The old man is not simply bound,—he is cast out with all his goods. There is not merely a calm, emotionless surrender of ourselves,—a "laying of our all upon the altar," but there is a dying out of self which can no more take place without deep emotion, than can natural death come upon a strong man without painful struggles. The animal life does not contend more stoutly with the king of terrors, than does the sinful life with the King of grace. The old man does not die until compelled to. The death struggles, whether more or less protracted, are real, and not imaginary or figurative. Paul said, "I am crucified with Christ;" and so does every one say, who has experienced inward holiness. But crucifixion is death, and a painful death. No one can give up all his cherished plans, and dearest associations, to follow Christ fully in the path of humility, reproaches, persecutions and afflictions, without a pang. When he makes this surrender, he will know it. But it must be made, if the joys of full salvation would be experienced.

When sinful self ceases to live, then Christ comes in and takes possession. The heart emptied of sin, is filled with the Spirit. A peace, which passeth all understanding, continually reigns. The ransomed believer now rejoices in Christ with "joy unspeakable, and full of glory." No words can express the rapture of his soul. Standing upon the tops of the mountains, where he is fanned by the breezes of Paradise, and ravished by a sight of the celestial city, he shouts aloud the praises of God; or, lying low in the valley of humility, he feels

> "A sacred awe that does not move,
> And all the silent heaven of love."

His heart is full of gratitude and praise, and out of the abundance of his heart, his mouth speaketh.

There is, we are aware, an experience called holiness, very different from this. The professor, in nine cases out of ten, one who has lost his first love, and who, therefore, needs to repent like any other sinner, is persuaded that he needs the blessing of holiness. He is told to deliberately consecrate himself to the Lord,—to "lay all upon the altar." When this is done, he is taught that he must believe, upon the authority of God's word, that the sacrifice is now accepted; that "the altar sanctifies the gift," and that he now enjoys the blessing of holiness. If he urges that he does not feel any different,—that he has not experienced any change, he is assured that he must live by faith and not by feeling,—that he must honor God by believing His word. The next and last step is to make a profession of holiness, and this must be kept up henceforth. Such a process, involving no mortification of pride, but rather gratifying it by giving one a reputation for piety, becomes popular wherever presented. Many pass through it, profess holiness, and deceive themselves to their soul's undoing. They say they are "rich, and increased with goods, and have need of nothing;" when, in reality, they are "poor and miserable, and blind and naked." They are as full of self as ever, conformed to the world, willing to receive honor of men, and ready to compromise whenever fashion demands it. They wink at popular sins, or boldly apoligize for them. We have seen such men, with their golden spectacles, and gold or silver headed canes, shutting out of meetings for holiness all testimony against slavery in the church,—and women adorned in "gold, or pearls, or costly array," pleading for worldly conformity, because their hearts are set upon these things!

Such persons enjoy holiness? Why, according to the Methodist standard,—and such are found among Methodists,—they are not scripturally awakened, much less converted or sanctified!

The "General Rules" of Methodism say that "we know that God's Spirit writes on truly awakened hearts," the necessity of avoiding evil of every kind, especially that which is most generally practiced, such as "Laying up treasure on earth,"—but these would make gain of godliness; "Softness and needless self-indulgence," —but these indulge self, in eating, drinking, dress, and conversation; "Reading those books that do not tend to the knowledge or love of God," such as novels, and the light literature of the day; "The putting on of gold and costly apparel,"—but these say their "conscience does not condemn them" for doing so. Yet, you profess holiness! Why, according to the standard of your own church, you are yet an unawakened sinner! You may occupy a high official or social position,—may have written a book on the subject of holiness,—you may be justly entitled to the gratitude and respect of the church, but all this does not prove that you are now in a state of salvation. If you do not "deny yourself and take up your cross daily, submitting to bear the reproach of Christ, to be as the filth and offscouring of the world, and looking that men should say all manner of evil of you falsely, for the Lord's sake," you have not, the Methodist Discipline says, "really fixed in your soul," even "a desire to flee from the wrath to come, and to be saved from your sins!" This is the decision which Methodism pronounces upon your condition. And is it not the Bible view of the case? Has not the light that was in thee become darkness? O, be honest with yourself! You confess to a loss of power. This is so striking that, blinded as you are, you cannot fail to perceive it. But if the power is gone, the purity is gone, the Holy Ghost, the sanctifier, is gone! Rouse from this state of stupid insensibility. Bewail your loss. Humble yourself deeply before God. Obtain pardon while you may. Then press on to full salvation. Remember that, "Without holiness no man shall see the Lord." Resolve to have the real thing if it takes your life. There is an awful warning to those who have been living in the way of salvation, and have enjoyed many works of the Divine favor, and are full of honors, in the record that is given of one, once a favorite of heaven. "It came to pass, that when Solomon was old, that his wives turned away his heart after other gods: and his heart was not perfect with the Lord his God."—I Kings 11:4.

CHAPTER XXIII.

A POWERLESS PROFESSION.

YOU profess holiness, but do you really enjoy perfect love? A profession of holiness without love is like a well without water, like a stove without fire, like a tree without fruit. It raises expectations only to disappoint them. You let down your bucket for water—it comes up empty. You go for warmth but find none. You shake the tree for fruit but gather nothing but leaves.

If your experience is a fruitless one, the fault is not in your circumstances but in your experience. You may be a pattern of plainness and non-conformity to the world—you may be uncompromising in your opposition to its fashions and pleasures—Zeno, the Stoic, was all this, and yet he was only a heathen, and not a Christian. But you cannot be filled with love to God and man without being a blessing to others. Toward those who are striving to do God's will you will have no feeling of envy or jealousy. You will not try to cripple their influence by lowering them in the estimation of others. You will rejoice with them that do rejoice. If they build faster or better than you, if you have love, you will not stop work and go to persecuting them on that account. If they really cast out devils in the name of Jesus, you will not forbid them, though they follow not you. "Love envieth not."—I Cor. 13:4.

Towards those who are out of the way you will feel—not anger—but compassion. Suppose they do act wrong, what else could you expect? You will not hold them off, nor act distant, as though you feared they might pollute you. Jesus came to *seek and to save them that are lost.* If you have His love you will go after those who go astray. We ask you again, Have you perfect love? Read its characteristics in the thirteenth chapter of 1st Corinthians. Ask yourself the question, as you read them one by one, Is this true of my experience? Am I able to suffer long and be kind? Am I free from envy and vanity? Do I not think better of those who think well of me, than I do of others of equal worth? Does not my opinion of others depend very much on the degree of attention which they pay to me?

A want of usefulness is an unerring sign of a want of love. Admit the fact. Stop blaming others. Quit finding fault.

Some preachers when they see a weakness among their people, give strong doses when they ought to take one first themselves. Get a real—not affected—love for souls, then your plain dealing will draw them to you, instead of driving them away. Then you can, in meekness, instruct those who oppose themselves, and God may give them repentance to the acknowledging of the truth.

Seek then, first of all, for a baptism of pure, *perfect love* upon your soul. Do not think you have it when the fruits are wanting. Own your need and then you will ask earnestly to have it supplied. God is ready to shed abroad His love in your heart by the Holy Ghost given unto you. For this, in the work of God, there can be no substitute. Increase of zeal may help somewhat —but nothing will fit you to live right and to do the good you may, but the fullness of the love of God. Do not, then, go another day without it. Is consecration needed to obtain it? Then make the consecration without delay. Keep back nothing. Let God have all. Present your body a living sacrifice. Let your talents, your time, your property, your all be at the disposal of Him to whom you belong.

Is confession called for? Have you manifested to others an unlovely disposition, contrary to the Spirit of Christ? The confession should be as broad as the offense. It may be in the family —it may be to those who look up to you, that you have exhibited your lack of the "love that beareth all things, that endureth all things," but no matter; make the confession humbly, and plainly, and without any excuses, and see how God will melt your heart and fill you with His love.

Be decided upon this point. Neglect what you may, do not put off seeking the fullness of the love of God. If you have ten talents it will enable you to use them to the glory of God;—if you have but one it will enable you to make the most of that, and secure to you your eternal reward when the work of life is done.

CHAPTER XXIV.

KINDS OF HOLINESS.

THE Scriptures teach that there are two kinds of holiness,—*true* and *false*. (Eph. 4:24.)

True holiness, wherever found, is essentially the same.

In matters not essential there may be a wide difference, but in the essentials there is agreement. An English sovereign and an American eagle were not cast in the same mold and have different inscriptions, but the metal of which they are composed is the same. One could be easily converted into the other. Whatever form gold is made to assume it retains its qualities. So, *true holiness* has, among all people, and in all ages, the same characteristics.

It is the work of the Holy Spirit. No education however Scriptural, no training however religious, can produce it. He who is truly holy is sanctified by the Holy Ghost. He has ceased from his own works. As God works in him he works out his own salvation. Hence, since true holiness has nothing in it of human merit, it is always found in connection with deep humility. There is nothing of self in it, and it does not seek self-glorification in any form.

This humility is manifested in every manner. Its possessor dresses plain. Nothing is worn for show or ornament. It cannot be told from the appearance of a soldier in the ranks whether he is rich or poor, so the dress of a saint does not indicate his temporal condition. He is unassuming, not claiming superiority over others.

Another element of true holiness is an all-absorbing love for God and man. God is loved, adored, obeyed. Man is loved as the image of God, the representative of Christ, and however fallen he may be, he is pitied, instructed, helped and elevated.

True holiness is obtained through faith in God, and it is never separated from an unwavering trust in Him. The car separated from the locomotive on an up-hill grade soon loses its motion in the right direction, and begins to run down hill; the soul which lets go its hold of God by unbelief, loses holiness, falls into sin, either of the heart, or life, or both, and takes the downward track to perdition.

False holiness may be classed under several heads.

There is an aristocratic, self-indulgent holiness. It gives its influence to build up fine, costly

KINDS OF HOLINESS.

houses of worship, with popular preachers, choir singing, select congregations from which the poor are excluded as regular attendants, by selling or renting the seats. It puts on airs, dresses sufficiently in style to make the impression that it does not belong to the common people. It seeks the society of the upper classes, and endeavors to explain away the requirements of the Gospel to suit their tastes. It goes as far in self-indulgence as public sentiment will permit. Tertullian, about the year A. D. 207, in cutting irony, refers to this class of holiness professors. "Who, among you, is superior in holiness, except him who is more frequent in banqueting, most sumptuous in catering, more learned in cups? Men of soul and flesh alone as you are, justly do you reject things spiritual." This kind of holiness is not generally persecuted by the world. If it is, it is ready to apologize, and to put on a less offensive form.

There is a fanatical holiness. It lays the greatest stress upon that for which it has the least reason and Scripture for its support. Its self-denial is great, and is only equalled by its self-will. It has in it an element of sincerity, but it is vitiated by being consecrated to its own will, rather than to the will of God. It lacks the great quality of submission. It does not know how to yield, even in matters the smallest and most indifferent. It must have its own way in every thing. Every one must submit to its dictation or receive its fiery denunciation.

There is a covetous holiness. It wears cheap clothing, but it is to avoid expense. It has sharp criticisms for every project that calls for an expenditure of money; but it is because it is unwilling to bear its part. It may have little, or it may have much, but what it has it holds on to with a miser's grasp. Frequently it opposes all church organizations, really because it wishes for some excuse for refusing to support them. It is mighty at tearing down—it never tries its hand at building up. It may burn palaces—it cannot rear a hovel.

See to it then that you have true holiness. Let your consecration be to God. Give yourself up for a habitation of the Holy Spirit. Let Him lead you into all truth. Let the Ten Commandments and the Sermon on the Mount be as much to you as "the exceeding great and precious promises." Let them dove-tail together in your experience.

Take pains o be clothed with humility. It is not enough not to feel proud, you should not look proud. Be of an humble spirit, then every thing about you will show forth that spirit.

Whatever you lack, do not lack that sanctification "without which no man shall see the Lord."—Heb. 12:14.

If you are without it be in haste to obtain it.

There is no time to be lost. Eternity is at hand. The great preparation for it is true holiness. It must be obtained here. The death-bed may be too late. Consecrate yourselves fully to God. Obey the leadings of the Spirit. Make every confession He prompts you to make. Take any position He directs you to take. Trust fully in Christ. Rely on Him. Believe His every promise, but, above all, believe in Him.

CHAPTER XXV.

DEFECTIVE HOLINESS.

HOLINESS belongs especially to the Lord. In Him it is pure, unmixed and underived. Hence He is called THE HOLY ONE, as if the name Holy and God are the same. "They have provoked the Holy One of Israel."—Isa. 1:4. "But shall stay upon the LORD, the Holy One of Israel."—Isa. 10:20. The Messiah in like manner is called the Holy One. "Neither wilt thou suffer thine Holy One to see corruption."—Ps. 16:10. "I know thee who thou art; the Holy One of God."—Luke 4:34.

Holiness in man is often defective. It may be wanting in some of its essential elements. Hence in the Scriptures we find some qualifying terms applied to holiness when used in connection with human beings. "Put on the new man, which after God is created in righteousness and true holiness."—Eph. 4:24. This implies that there is a false holiness—that which passes for holiness though wanting in some of its essential properties.

"That we being delivered out of the hand of

our enemies might serve him without fear, in holiness and righteousness before him, all the days of our life."—Luke 1:74, 75. The phrase, "before him," is the highest form of a superlative, and denotes a holiness and righteousness which will bear the scrutiny of God's all-searching eye.

The holiness of the day is so ineffective because so much of it is defective. The load does not move because so much of the steam is lost. The medicine does not cure because it is combined with so many neutralizing substances. The gold is not current because mixed with so much alloy. Let us see to it that we have true holiness.

Much of the current holiness is wanting in spirituality. It has a worldly aspect. Generally it talks after a worldly manner. It keeps up a profession of holiness where it is popular to profess holiness. But in general its conversation is of the earth, earthy. It lacks the odor of sanctity. It does not bear the solemn, heavenly aspect of one who holds communion with God. Notwithstanding its efforts to the contrary it carries it with it and diffuses wherever it goes a worldly spirit.

Much of it is wanting in loyalty to God. While God is nominally acknowledged as Sovereign, the supreme allegiance is given to self, or to society, or to the church. Some yield to the claims of holiness until they appear to interfere with their worldly interest. They give a positive testimony to holiness until they discover that some whose good opinion they covet treat them with coldness in consequence. Then they are guarded or silent. They set out to meet the requirements of the Bible on dress; but when they find it brings upon them reproach and persecution, they go with the multitude and are conformed to this world.

Some meet the requirements of holiness as far as they can and keep in harmony with the authorities of the church. They have their convictions clear and positive. As far as the usages of the church are in harmony with these convictions, they stand by them firmly. But let them be expressed ever so plainly in the standards of church doctrine, yet if the church disregards them in practice, they readily fall in with it and act directly contrary to the clearest convictions that God gives them. A wealthy member of the M. E. Church saw clearly that the practice of renting or selling seats in the house of worship is contrary to the Scriptures. They needed a new church. He was asked to head the subscription. He offered to if they would make the seats free. The preacher insisted they could not build a free-seated church. The Christian man offered to build one himself if they would make the seats free. His offer was accepted and he built, a large, convenient church. Only a few years elapsed before the preachers persuaded him to consent to rent the seats in that very church.

By artful management the most iniquitous decisions are obtained in the church tribunals against some of its most devoted and godly ministers. Men claiming to be advocates of holiness, who would have defended these proscribed ones if they had chanced to be in a majority, close their ears to the strongest testimony, and give to the merest phantoms of the imagination all the authority of Sacred Writ. A holiness that ignores the claims of justice only as they are sanctioned by the majority, a holiness that acknowledges no higher fealty than loyalty to the church, that makes it its highest duty to stand by those in power, do what they may, is treason to God. It is a refined, subtle idolatry—but an idolatry not less damning than that which leads its votaries to bow down to stocks and stones. A saint yields his highest allegiance to God. Truth and justice he recognizes as attributes of God, and however they may be trampled in the dust he knows he cannot be false to them and at the same time be true to God.

It was this disposition to stand by the truth of God in each other when the authorities of church and state were arrayed against it, that made the primitive Christians invincible. Paul writes, "But call to remembrance the former days, in which, after ye were illuminated, ye endured a great fight of afflictions; partly whilst ye were made a gazing stock both by reproaches and afflictions; and partly, whilst ye became companions of them that were so used. For ye had compassion of me in my bonds, and took joyfully the spoiling of your goods, knowing in yourselves that ye have in heaven a better and an enduring substance."—Heb. 10:32-34.

Lucian was a celebrated Greek writer and an enemy of the Christian religion. He flourished about the year of our Lord 176. In speaking of Christians he says: "It is incredible what expedition they use when any of their friends are in trouble. In a word they spare nothing upon such an occasion; for these miserable men have no doubt they shall be immortal and live forever; therefore they contemn death, and many surrender themselves to sufferings. Moreover their first law-giver has taught them, that they are all brethren, when they have turned and renounced the gods of the Greeks, and worship that Master of theirs who was crucified, and engage to live according to His laws. They have a sovereign contempt for all the things of this world, and look upon them as common."

If this doctrine of supreme loyalty to the church had prevailed in our Saviour's time, Christianity could never have been established. For Christ was crucified by the authorities of the church: and that too, not by one church among many, but at the instigation of the chief priests of the only church of God then on the earth—a church founded by Abraham and sanctioned by the working among them from age to age of wonders and miracles, and made rich by the wisdom and illustrious by the piety of prophets whom God raised up among them from time to time.

If loyalty to the church be our first duty, then were Luther and Wesley heretics and schismatics and not the reformers we are accustomed to consider them. The very foundation principle of the reformation is, that every soul owes its first and highest allegiance to God. On no other principle can the reformation be defended.

Preachers and churches are helps in their appropriate places; but when they require one to do what God forbids, then, cost what it may, God must have the preference.

If masonry be, as is clearly shown by the late President Finney, by President Blanchard and others, and in our tract entitled "False Religion," a rival and hostile religion to Christianity, then that holiness is defective which closes its eyes to this great fact and sustains Masonic preachers in its churches.

If selling or renting pews in houses of worship is a plain violation of the prohibition to have respect of persons in seating congregations, and is contrary to the spirit and teaching of the Gospel, then that holiness is defective which gives its sanction or support to this anti-Christian practice.

If the Bible requires plainness of dress and forbids Christians to adorn themselves with "braided hair or gold or pearls or costly array," then is that holiness defective which pays no attention to these plain commands, but conforms to the fashions of the world in things plainly forbidden by the Word of God.

CHAPTER XXVI.

FALSE HOLINESS.

IT is a false holiness, which is built upon a false assumption. "Sanctify them through thy truth."—John 17:17. It is a false assumption which takes it for granted that those who maintain a respectable standing in a respectable Church are therefore justified. Some of them are. Many are not. "By their fruits ye shall know them."—Matt. 7:20. Some love the world. They do not attempt to conceal it. "If any man love the world, the love of the Father is not in him."—I John 2:15. They seek the friendship of the world. For this purpose they enter into voluntary associations of a purely worldly character. They give these the preference over the Church of Christ. They are found at the lodge more frequently than at the prayer-meeting. "Ye adulterers and adulteresses, know ye not that the friendship of the world is enmity with God? whosoever therefore will be a friend of the world is the enemy of God."—Jas. 4:4.

People of this class need pardon first. They are under condemnation—and should be led to see it—*for* they walk not after the Spirit, but after the flesh. If they have ever been in the way of life they have erred from the truth. They must be converted. (Jas. 5:19). To encourage them to think that they are in a state of salvation, is to encourage them to believe a lie. To build a structure of holiness on this foundation is doing a work that in all probability will not stand. Those who are honest, finding that they have not received the blessing which they thought they did receive, will be quite likely to conclude that all is delusion. Those who are not honest will gladly take up with the delusion, and may hold on to it till they die, to their eternal undoing.

Live holiness! Talk holiness! Preach holiness! If souls who are under condemnation are truly awakened by the Spirit, they will, even though they go forward for holiness, soon begin to pray for pardon. Encourage them to go on with this prayer until it is answered. Do not try to persuade them that they are better off than the Spirit shows them that they are. Let them go to the bottom, and confess all that God shows them they ought to confess. Let them seek until the Spirit answers to the blood, and tells them they are born of God. Having obtained pardon for sin, and victory over sin, they will be in a condition to go forward and seek *true holiness*. They will not feel like closing their eyes to the light, and make popular usage a substitute for the word of God. The fullest consecration which the Spirit demands will be cheerfully made. They will not consecrate up to the point of popularity and stop there—nor up to the point of loyalty to the Church and stop there. Where the Holy Ghost leads they will cheerfully follow. They will not close their eyes to popular sins, under the pretence that they do not understand them—they will not hesitate to espouse the right because they stand alone.

It is a false holiness which takes the courage all out of a man and makes him the supple tool of the artful and the designing. The religious instincts of a soul truly saved of God are a safer guide for him than the logic of others. He wants to know what God would have him know. He wants to stand where God would have him stand.

That we are in danger of taking up with a false holiness, is clearly implied in many passages of the Scriptures. The Apostle's expression "True holiness," implies that there is a false. The numerous exhortations against being deceived, also imply this.

Be careful then, as you prize the salvation of your soul, and do not take up with a false holiness. Buy, at any cost, the "gold tried in the fire."

Do not countenance the promotion of false

holiness. Examine carefully the character of the preaching which you support, and of the books and periodicals which you circulate. Give your endorsement to nothing that will not stand the test of the judgment day. Be decided on this point. Take your stand for a genuine work. The necessity is laid upon us.

"For we can do nothing against the truth, but for the truth."—II Cor. 13:8.

There is no end to counterfeits. As soon as one is exposed, another is put into circulation. It is so in the financial world; it is so in the religious world. But there is this difference, no one wishes to take a bad dollar, while the great majority appear to prefer a bad religion. The crowds which go to hear Mr. Moody, appear to think they have done well if they go to hear him without paying any thing; while of the crowd that goes to hear Mr. Ingersoll blaspheme, each individual will pay his half dollar, or dollar, without complaining.

A few years ago it was the fashion to fight holiness. It is now becoming the fashion to preach holiness. But there is a great difference in the kind of holiness preached. All is not gold that glitters. All is not holiness that passes for it. There is still what the Apostle calls "true holiness;" and there is a false holiness.

We went to hear one of the divines in attendance upon the Prophetic Conference lately held in Chicago, preach on "Sanctification." It was an able, exhaustive sermon. The whole tenor of it was false and flattering. It assumed that the whole meaning of the term was being "set apart for holy purposes." Thus the place where sacrifices were offered was a holy place; the altar was sanctified; the first born were sanctified. But he said their character was not changed. "So," he said, to a fashionable congregation, "if you are believers, *you are sanctified*, you may be the subjects of infirmities; you may fail in a thousand things, but your sanctification is complete. You are complete in Christ." This, he maintained, is the *condition of* all believers. But it implies no change in their characters.

They should strive to have their character and conduct correspond to their condition. If they persevered they would improve, but they could never attain in this life the perfection which God requires.

The preacher said that Finney and Mahan, and even John Wesley had lowered the standard. "God," the preacher said, "requires of man nothing less than absolute perfection."

Is it not strange that, with an open Bible before them, men dare preach such doctrines? Under the Old Dispensation, a prophet asked, "And what doth the Lord require of thee but to do justly and to love mercy, and to walk humbly with thy God?"—Micah 6:8.

So Jesus gives, as the great commandment, "Thou shalt love the Lord thy God with all thy heart, and with all thy soul, and with all thy mind."—Matt. 22:37. This is plain. It is as reasonable as it is plain. "With all thy heart"—not with the heart of an archangel—not even with the heart of a superior human being—but "with all thy heart." The weakest, the most ignorant can do that. The strongest, the most gifted can do nothing more. This is what the Bible means by our being sanctified. It is loving God with all our heart and soul and mind.

But, that sanctification is not merely a change in our condition or relation but also a change in our nature, in our character and conduct, the Scriptures plainly teach.

Take one plain passage, "And the very God of peace sanctify you wholly; and I pray God your whole spirit and soul and body be preserved blameless unto the coming of our Lord Jesus Christ. Faithful is he that calleth you, who also will do it."—I Thess. 5:23, 24.

This passage carefully considered throws much light upon the subject of sanctification. It teaches

1. That souls at conversion are sanctified, but not *wholly*.

2. That entire sanctification is subsequent to justification. They were already justified.

3. That entire sanctification is God's work—a work done in us by God's Spirit.

4. That it brings soul and body and spirit into a blameless condition; for they cannot be preserved blameless until they are first made blameless.

5. That it is attainable, for God is to do it. Who will dare limit the power of His grace?

6. That entire sanctification is attainable *now*, in this life, for the Apostle prays that we may be preserved in this state.

7. That it is a state from which one need never fall. For the Apostle prays that we may be preserved in this state unto "the coming of our Lord Jesus Christ." And he adds "Faithful is he that calleth you who also will do it." Only do your part and God will do His. There is not a single doubt about it.

Such is a brief outline of the teaching of one plain passage on this subject.

Those who profess to be looking for the second, personal coming of Christ should be careful that they do not themselves furnish an evidence that it is near at hand by "having a form of godliness, but denying the power thereof."

While we look for Christ's second, personal coming we should go to work with awe-inspiring earnestness to get ourselves, and as many others as we can, prepared for His kingdom and His coming.

Especially should we put forth definite, well-directed efforts to spread every where the doctrine and the experience of that "holiness without which no man shall see the Lord."--Heb. 12:14.

CHAPTER XXVII.

A FIGHTING HOLINESS.—"SANCTIFICATION IN STREAKS."

WE do not mean those who fight holiness, but use the word fighting as an adjective to describe holiness.

The phrase may be used in a bad sense and a good sense.

A professor of religion who is all alive to his own importance, ready to join issue with everybody on every occasion who differs with him, to put the worst construction upon the actions and the worst meaning to the words of others, who stirs up strife and divisions wherever he goes, has a bad kind of warring holiness. He may be zealous to reform yet does but little towards promoting "on earth peace, and good will toward men." He is very apt to substitute bitterness for love, presumption for faith, obstinacy for firmness. Men who are naturally pugnacious, even when truly sanctified, are liable to lose the fullness of love, and then become quarrelsome: and if, as is generally the case, they keep up their profession of holiness, they prejudice sensible people against the doctrine, and do a vast amount of harm.

But true holiness is not the easy, obsequious, compromising principle that many appear to think that it is, It is brave as a hero and at the same time gentle as a woman. It is valiant for the truth. When called upon, it is ready to defend it, and if need be to die for it. The man of God is solemnly charged—"Fight the good fight of faith, lay hold on eternal life."—I Tim. 6:12. Our Lord says, "Think not that I am come to send peace on earth: I came not to send peace, but a sword."—Matt. 10:34. Wherever sin and true holiness come in contact there must be war.

All eminent saints have been great warriors. Paul describes his life at its close by saying, "I have fought a good fight." Luther and Wesley and Finney were mighty men of war.

But see to it that in the midst of all your fightings you keep filled with love.

We have a Presbyterian brother—a devout man of God, and an able preacher—who holds to the doctrine of sanctification. He says that, as a matter of fact, he finds that those professing holiness are generally "sanctified in streaks." Is there not too much ground for this observation?

Some evidently love the world. They gain all they can, and save all they can,—but they do not give all they can. They have enough, and more than enough, to make themselves and those dependent on them comfortable as long as they live. Still they go on laying up for themselves "treasures on earth." Some make a gain of godliness. Even "holiness camp-meetings" are so managed that a good deal of money is made out of them. The ground for tents to stand on is rented at a large profit; the tents and furniture are rented at a profit; and even the railroads—grasping as are these corporations—are made to share with the managers, the profits of carrying the worshipers to these great gatherings. If those who labor specially to promote holiness set such an example of money-making, is it to be wondered at if the same spirit should be imbibed by others?

Some are greatly wanting in meekness and humility. They put on style. In their dress, they violate the plain rules of Scripture. They mince their words, and affect a high degree of social refinement in their manner of speaking.

Others are too forward. They never know their place. If they cannot lead, they balk. They must be foremost, or they will not work at all. If you disagree with them in opinion, they take it that you are their enemy. An effort to correct anything that is really objectionable, they count as persecution. They are not "easy to be entreated."

Some are wanting in self-denial. They live in

ease and self-indulgence. They do not seem to know what it is to deny themselves of anything for Jesus' sake.

Beloveds, the Gospel proposes to effect in each one of us a perfect cure. We are sanctified "through the truth."—John 17:17. This cannot be too strongly impressed upon the mind. You will be sanctified only so far as you receive the truth. If your views of truth are defective or distorted, there will be a corresponding defect or distortion in your piety. Do not be rickety Christians, with a head disproportioned to the rest of your body. SEARCH THE SCRIPTURES.— Aim at a full and harmonious development of all the Christian graces. If you find you are defective in any respect, do not peevishly throw away the whole of your experience, and go over the same old, beaten road again, but come to God for that particular grace. Persevere in prayer until you get it. Insist upon it that it is your privilege to be right with God in all respects. Be willing to know your faults; for until you know them you will never seek deliverance from them. Welcome the light.

"And beside this, giving all diligence, add to your faith virtue; and to virtue knowledge; and to knowledge temperance; and to temperance patience; and to patience godliness; and to godliness brotherly kindness; and to brotherly kindness, charity."—II Pet. 1:5-7.

CHAPTER XXVIII.

HOLINESS BEFORE THE LORD.

EVERYTHING valuable has its counterfeit. Mock marriages, spurious medicines, base coins, have always deceived many, and yielded a harvest of sorrow in place of looked-for joy.

Holiness is an attribute of God. It is an essential attribute. It is the want of holiness which makes Satan the devil.

Holiness is the great want of man. Without it he cannot go to a Heaven which sin never defiles, and whose every inhabitant is holy. No degree of talent, no amount of learning, no abundance of riches can compensate for the want of holiness.

It is not then wonderful that Satan, transformed into an angel of light, should bend all his energies to produce a close imitation of holiness. He succeeds so admirably that he would deceive, if possible, the very elect.

The Scriptures give us plain warning. If we take any counterfeit, however spurious, for genuine holiness, ours is the fault, and the resulting loss. At the very opening of the Gospel we are put upon our guard. Zacharias, filled with the Spirit, blessed God for the coming of Christ to perform the mercy promised to our fathers; "The oath which he sware to our father Abraham, that he would grant unto us, that we being delivered out of the hand of our enemies might serve him without fear, in holiness and righteousness before him, all the days of our life."—Luke 1:73-75. The phrase "before God" is a superlative expression, and denotes that whatever it is applied to is really and truly what it appears to be. God sees through all disguises. He is never deceived. So when the sacred writers wish to express that which is true and real they use the phrase, "before God." Thus it is said, "The earth also was corrupt before God."—Gen. 6:11. That is, it was thoroughly and generally corrupt. Of Zacharias and Elizabeth it is said, "They were both righteous before God."—Luke 1:6. They were really and consistently righteous. So the phrase "holiness and righteousness before the Lord" implies that there is a holiness that will not bear the inspection of God's all-searching eye. The same idea is conveyed by Paul, "Put on the new man, which after God is created in righteousness and true holiness."—Eph. 4:24. Why this qualifying word "true?" The inspired writers do not use such terms at random. "True holiness" implies that there is a false. This is evident. The Scriptures then put us on our guard. We must, therefore, examine carefully the holiness teachings which seek our approval. Are they in harmony with the teachings of the Bible? They may be in some respects and yet be radically wrong. The doctrines we receive are the invisible chains that bind us to a life of faith and obedience. But a chain is no stronger than its weakest link. So, much that passes for holiness will be found defective in the day when its strength is tested.

This defective holiness is rapidly on the increase. It is becoming popular. It excites little opposition, provokes little persecution.

1. Bible holiness implies a settled hatred of sin. A holy person puts away all sin. He gives it no countenance, either in himself or others. And he calls that sin which God calls sin. No one says, "I will go and commit some sin against God." But he does something which God says he must not do, or he neglects to do something which God says he must do. Talk about consecrating some favorite idol to the Lord! God says put it away. You may consecrate as much as you please, but God will have nothing to do with it. The goodly Babylonish garment and the wedge of gold he will not accept even if consecrated.

God says, "Whose adorning let it not be that outward adorning of plaiting the hair, and of wearing of gold, or putting on of apparel."— I Pet. 3:3. Many holiness teachers not only do not enforce this command, but they set the example of its open violation. We have seen gentlemen holiness teachers with ornaments of gold plainly in view; and lady teachers waving ostrich plumes upon their bonnets. Yet they make a very strong profession of being saved from sin. But the trouble is they do not call it sin to break a plain command of the Bible which it is popular to break. Their rule of conduct is, not the word of God, but the usages of what is called good society. According to their method of teaching, the Bible must be construed, no matter what violence is done to its language, so as not to offend the popular sentiment. This quality that aims to please, and never to give offence, that suppresses in religious gatherings all plain testimony against worldly conformity in dress or needless worldly associations, by joining secret societies, may appear amiable and attractive; but it is not Bible holiness. To call it so is misleading. Its proper name is politeness, and not holiness. Well-bred people of the world act in the same way when it does not conflict with their interests. Understand us. We do not say that this easy complacency is all wrong. In a worldly sense it may do good. It smooths much of the asperity of daily life. It is as oil to lessen the friction which results from the intercourse of persons of opposite views and conflicting interests. But it is not Bible holiness. It is wanting in the fundamental element—that love for God which leads one to obey all his commands. It fatally mistakes a love of popularity for the love of God. This is not the holiness of George Fox and John Wesley and Charles G. Finney. These men of God bore clear, ringing testimonies against popular sins. Theirs was not that complaisant, man-pleasing spirit that fears to offend the world. They gave no quarters to popular sin.

2. Bible holiness implies that the heart is filled with love—genuine love to God and man. It reproves, but it does it in the spirit of meekness. It bears an out-and-out testimony against popular sins, but it does it in kindness and not in anger; for conscience sake and not to gratify a spirit of resentment.

The great skill of the deceiver is shown in pushing earnest souls in to the one extreme or the other. Some of the zealous advocates of holiness not only reprove sin but they undertake to anathematize all who dare to disagree with them. To oppose their course they call fighting against God. Let one do it ever so mildly and he is assailed by the most opprobrious epithets they can use. This furious zeal they call holiness. And the strangest part of it is they get some honest souls to accept their leadership and indorse all they do and say. These fierce propagandists, with tongues and pens like a sharp two-edged sword, manifest a spirit that we would look for rather among the devotees of Islam than among the followers of Christ.

A holy person does not indulge in fierce vituperation and denunciation. He is uncompromising—but at the same time gentle and kind.

Let us then see to it that we walk blameless in holiness "before the Lord." Deception can be of no avail. At the best it is short-lived. We shall soon enter upon a world of stern realities. We shall, whatever estimate we put upon ourselves, be weighed in the undeviating balances of God's sanctuary. Let us see to it that we be not found wanting.

CHAPTER XXIX.

PROMOTING HOLINESS.

THAT the work of holiness is gaining ground in this country is, we think, evident. The labors of those engaged in promoting it are meeting with some encouragement. Yet but little is done in comparison of what ought to be done. What is the reason?

One prominent reason is, that in most of the churches the people are taught that they can be saved without holiness. This is not done in so many words. That would startle the hearers. But the people are made to believe that they will go to Heaven, if they join the church and are loyal to it, even though they continue to live in sin. Men desire to gain advantages on the easiest terms. If two articles, in every respect of equal value, are offered for sale, the one for which the lowest price is asked is sold first. When people who love the world, its fashions, its associations, its honors, its pleasures, are assured that they can gain Heaven, by paying the preacher and supporting the church, and still hold on to their cherished sins, they naturally choose this course.

We must show that no one can be saved who is not so far made holy that he stops committing sin. "He that committeth sin is of the devil."—I John 3:8. This we must insist on. And also "Whosoever is born of God doth not commit sin."—I John 3:9. Those who are made to believe that they can be good Christians and at the same time live in sin do not desire to become holy. Why should they, if they can at the same time enjoy the pleasures of sin and reap the rewards of holiness? We must remove this delusion from the minds of the people. We must show that the popular religion of the day is not true Christianity. It takes courage to do this in a proper manner. It must not be done in a way to create the impression that we are making war upon the churches. This would stir up resistance.

There must be nothing belligerent or pharisaical in our manner. We must do it in the spirit in which Paul wrote of the carnal professors of his time. "For many walk, of whom I have told you often, and now tell you even weeping, that they are the enemies of the cross of Christ; whose end is destruction, whose god is their belly, and whose glory is in their shame, who mind earthly things."—Phil. 3:18, 19. That this applies too generally to the members of popular churches, their pastors practically acknowledge, by getting up festivals and appealing to their appetites when they wish to raise money. There is a great difference in the effect between saying this in a harsh, censorious, upbraiding spirit, or saying it, as Paul did, with a tender heart, even weeping. It is a sad sight,—one to make angels weep,—to see pulpits and pews of professedly Christian churches filled with men and women who give the most unmistakable evidence of "minding earthly things"—of living in plain violation of the commands of God. But instead of crying "peace and safety" and representing to them that "if they go on they will finally get to Heaven," but they "need the blessing of holiness to make them more useful," we must show them tenderly but plainly from the word of God that *the end* of the course they are pursuing is destruction.

Where this is done in the Holy Ghost the work of holiness will go on in power. The people will be led to repent of their sins; and then go on "perfecting holiness in the fear of the Lord." They will get an experience that fills them with joy; and that will give them power over others.

But when in a church composed of backsliders and of those who never were converted, holiness is preached as a blessing that they may receive at once, by simply believing, the result is self-deception. Many profess entire holiness when at the utmost they have only obtained pardon.

They are urged to profess the highest state of sanctification when they are in the lowest state of justification. And some even become the advocates of holiness when, according to the standard laid down in the Bible and in the M. E. Discipline, they are not fully awakened. The sad sight is witnessed of men preaching holiness who are so defiled by tobacco that the pure shrink from coming near them, and of women, waving their plumes and flaunting their jewelry professing to be saved to the uttermost! This makes sensible people mistrustful of the doctrine.

To promote the work of holiness then, we must not close our eyes to this state of things, and act as if it did not exist. A doctor never cures the cholera by treating it as if it were only a slight irregularity. We must acknowledge the desperate state of the case and apply the proper remedy. It will of course stir up conflict, but we must meet it in the name of Jesus.

It is cowardly and criminal for the advocates of holiness to encourage professors in self-delusion. It is treason to Christ to persuade those who know they love the world, that they are in a state of salvation—weak it may be—to be pitied and petted, when they need to break down before God and seek forgiveness. Let us do thorough work for God. *"Cursed be he* that doeth the work of the LORD deceitfully."—Jer. 48:10.

The great hindrance to the work of holiness on

earth is man's depravity. This creates obstacles of every conceivable kind. This exists everywhere, wherever man is found. There is no avoiding it. No locality can be found in which the people are naturally inclined to follow holiness. No people have ever yet been discovered who welcomed the pure, unadulterated truth of God, and set themselves to work in obedience to its requirements. To induce depraved men to seek holiness they must be drawn from above by the Holy Spirit. Without this supernatural aid, the natural opposition of man to holiness will never be overcome.

Then, to successfully preach holiness, something more is needed than a correct understanding of the doctrine, and to possess the ability to state it clearly and defend it with unanswerable arguments. These are important. To embrace the truth, people need to see the truth. It is unreasonable to require a man to believe that which he does not comprehend with at least some clearness. So that advocates of holiness should take pains to acquaint themselves with the doctrine. They should avail themselves of the help of those who can afford them help. They should be able to bring forth a plain text of the Scriptures in confirmation of every statement of doctrine which they make.

But above all other qualifications, holiness teachers need to speak under a baptism of the

Holy Ghost. They should be divinely inspired. Their words should be in demonstration of the Spirit and in power. They should present the truth on fire. Without this, little more will be done than to convince the understanding. To move men to act, their hearts must be touched. Their consciences must be aroused. Argument alone will not do this. Noise will not do it. Quietness will not do it. The feelings of the speaker must be enlisted and warmed. Fire kindles fire. Life begets life. Then go before the people already warmed up. Especially if you design to say plain, pointed truths, get your heart filled with love. Melted ore melts ore. If the people are dead, the necessity is all the greater for you to have life, and to have it more abundantly. You cannot impart what you do not possess.

Do you design to attend camp-meetings to help on the work of God? Begin at once the needed preparation. Study those passages especially which speak of the work of the Spirit. Get thoroughly imbued with the idea of the great work the Holy Spirit can accomplish, if it is poured out upon the multitude. Read of the many who were pricked in the heart. Think of the improbable ones who were converted. The Holy Ghost has lost none of His power. He can still disturb Pharisees and awaken sinners, and stir up the lukewarm. What is needed to make camp-meetings a success, is the outpouring of the Spirit upon the people.

See how very few ever secure an outpouring of the Spirit on the many! When the wonderful results of the day of Pentecost were accomplished, there was in the large congregation but a small proportion of believers. But they were all filled with the Holy Ghost.

When duly impressed with the importance of having the Spirit, consider to whom it is promised, and on what easy conditions! The ignorant as well as the learned may be filled with the Spirit. There is one condition for all—obey God. "And we are his witnesses of these things: and so is also the Holy Ghost, whom God hath given to them that obey him."—Acts 5:32.

CHAPTER XXX.

HOLINESS OPPOSED.

TRUE holiness is not popular. Let one confine himself to that branch of holiness which consists in doing good to the bodies of men, and he will meet with general acceptance. After he is dead, all will unite to honor his name.

But let one take up another branch of holiness, and seek to do good to the souls of men, by conscientiously declaring to them the whole counsel of God, and he will not be popular. As a rule, he will be persecuted. Christ was persecuted; likewise Paul, so too Luther, John Wesley, and Jonathan Edwards also. Any man, at the present day, however gentle and prudent he may be, who insists that his hearers, to be saved, must forsake pride, and freemasonry, and all popular sins, and dress plain, and lead a self-denying life, will meet with opposition and persecution. The cross has not lost its reproach. The carnal mind has not become friendly to God. Righteousness has not come into fellowship with unrighteousness. Light does not enjoy communion with darkness even in this advanced age.

John A. Wood says in the *Christian Standard:*

"The conviction is pressed upon us, unwelcome as it may be, that there is opposition in the Church to Christian holiness, and that it to some extent, is on the increase. We had rather believe otherwise; but clear light and facts manifest on the subject are painfully convincing. We cannot hold our peace and see our Saviour dishonored by the guilt and shame of many of His professed friends. To be faithful to God and point out the faults of the Church is no evidence of being her enemy. 'He who tells me my faults is my friend.'

"It is easily seen that in the Church of to-day there is apathy, and more or less hostility, to holiness of heart and life. We know, and rejoice, there are many exceptions, but these are far from being general. Where there is no open hostility to the subject, there is a deep and all-pervading spiritual apathy and indifference regarding it.

"We ask: Why is this ? What are the causes of this state of things ? That Satan and wicked men should hate and oppose holiness is to be expected; but that men and women in the church of God, with baptismal, sacramental, and church vows upon them, should be indifferent to it, or oppose it, is surprising indeed. But there are causes for it, and one is the sad fact that there are many backsliders in the Church, and doubtless the same is true in the ministry.

"The main cause, as we view it, is the low standard of piety in the church generally. The degree of piety in many cases requisite for admission to the Church, and the amount requisite to sustain a fair standing in it, is fearfully small. It does not compare at all favorably with the piety of the New Testament, as drawn from its precepts or examples. Hence, when the Scripture doctrine of holiness is presented, it frequently meets with decided opposition.

"How much does the common standard in our churches include of self-denial, of cross-bearing, of deadness to the world, and of agonizing prayer? How much of daily labor for the salvation of souls? How much does it demand in the way of entire consecration of all we have, all we can do, and how much of our whole being to the cause and service of God?

"New Testament piety demands all these; but it would seem that they have largely dropped out of the elements of Christian character, and are not requisite now for Christian life. Though these items continue in our discipline and church-manuals, their spirit and meaning have gone, and left only the hollow-sounding names.

"When holiness, including all these and other essential items, is presented with clearness and power, it stirs up opposition. An Eastern doctor of divinity said not long since: 'I find something in me that kicks against this sanctification.'

Happy would it be for the Church of God if he were an exception.

"This low grade of piety is not Bible piety. The consecration so prevalent these days is not Bible consecration. The Bible gives no countenance to the idea that a partial consecration of one's self to God can be accepted. The Scripture delineation of real godliness gives no countenance to the easy, slipshod piety so prevalent. It gives no description of a second-rate piety which the Lord will accept as better than none. 'I know thy works, that thou art neither cold nor hot. I would thou wert either cold or hot. So then because thou art lukewarm and neither cold nor hot, I will spew thee out of my mouth.'

"In all periods of the Church, in modern times, there have been those who have tried to elevate the standard of piety to where the New Testament puts it, and these have always met a decided, and sometimes a bitter, opposition from the Church. Luther, Wesley, Edwards and Finney are prominent examples of this. The special advocates of holiness in this country— east and west, north and south—need no proof that there is opposition to this subject among professing Christians. The little, petty innuendoes, sneers, misrepresentations, and ostracism, to which they are subject, are all the proof that is necessary.

"Let any man have his heart filled with Gospel light, love, and power, and then, realizing the moral deficiency in the Church, labor directly to bring it up to a higher standard of piety, he will soon find a decided lack of sympathy, and a tide of opposition in the Church; and while he may labor wisely and carry the conviction of the Church with him, he will find all the depravity in the Church against him. Human depravity is always opposed to holiness."

CHAPTER XXXI.

JUSTIFICATION AND ENTIRE SANCTIFICATION DISCRIMINATED.

WRITES an intelligent, pious brother: "In I Cor. 1:2, Paul wrote 'To them that are sanctified in Christ Jesus.' In succeeding chapters he states that there were divisions among them, that they were babes in Christ, and that he had fed them with milk; and worse still, that there was even a case of incest among them. Now the argument is this, that he accuses these sanctified persons of things that a justified person could not do, therefore sanctification is less than justification. Please explain."

We answer—1. Paul does not speak of this person of whom he complains as either sanctified or justified. What he complains of is that the church allowed him a place among them. He commands them to withdraw their fellowship at once until the wicked man complained of is brought to repentance. " But now I have written unto you not to keep company, if any man that is called a brother be a fornicator, or covetous, or an idolater, or a railer, or a drunkard, or an extortioner, with such an one, no not to eat."—I Cor 5:11. Calling a man a "brother" does not make him a brother in Christ. When then, Paul speaks of the church at Corinth as sanctified, he speaks of it in its general character, and then points out the exceptions.

2. Every Christian is sanctified. Before he is converted he sanctifies himself; that is, sets himself apart to do God's service, to abandon sin and lead a holy life. When converted he is sanctified by the Spirit—is really made holy to that degree that he has victory over sin. He does not commit sin. "Whosoever is born of God doth not commit sin."—I John 3:9. This is a high state of grace. But it is not entire sanctification.

With the Thessalonians, Paul in his first epistle, finds no fault whatever. He speaks of them in terms of the highest commendation. Yet he prays for them. "And the very God of peace sanctify you wholly."—I Thess. 5:23. They were already sanctified in part. He prays that the work may be done for them by God—and does not tell them to look for it by a process of gradual development and growth. They already had a genuine conversion. They were active, zealous Christians, fit subjects for the blessing of holiness.

These two distinct works of grace are recognized also in the first Epistle to the Corinthians.

They were converted—sanctified in part—babes in Christ. But as there were strifes and divisions among them, they were not spiritual—not sanctified wholly—but carnal, and walked as men. (I Cor. 3:1, 3.)

The same idea is also expressed in Titus 3:5, 6: "Not by works of righteousness which we have done, but according to his mercy he saved us, by the washing of regeneration and renewing of the Holy Ghost which he shed on us abundantly, through Jesus Christ our Saviour." Here we have—1. The work of conversion expressed by "the washing of regeneration." 2. Of entire sanctification expressed by the "renewing of the Holy Ghost."

So also in II Peter 1:4: "Whereby are given unto us exceeding great and precious promises; that by these ye might be partakers of the divine nature, having escaped the corruption that is in the world through lust." Here is—1. Conversion—"having escaped the corruption," and 2. Entire sanctification—"partakers of the divine nature."

These two works are distinctly referred to in the Old as well as in the New Testament. Some get into perplexity by confounding sanctification with entire sanctification. We should be careful and not do it. By using Scriptural language in its proper connection, we avoid confusion and help to promulgate sound doctrine.

By seeking entire sanctification as a distinct blessing obtainable by faith we get it clear and definite, to the satisfying of the soul; while those who think they obtained all at conversion that God can give them, generally either go back, or go on in a manner unsatisfactory even to themselves. They very rarely can testify that the blood of Jesus Christ cleanses them from all sin. Their experience and their language are indefinite. But let them make a definite consecration, and pray definitely to be sanctified wholly, and the work will be done.

These are not so far apart as many imagine. They bear about the same relation to each other, that a weed cut off, does to a weed pulled up by the roots. The one may be compared to a piece of land just cleared off with the stumps still remaining, the other to a field from which every root has been extracted. Both bear fruit of an equally good quality, but the latter is more easily cultivated, and yields the more abundant harvest. The justified soul does not commit sin, but he feels sin still remaining, against which he is compelled to fight that he may retain the mastery. The sanctified soul is delivered from all evil tempers—no wrong temper—none contrary to love remains in the soul. All his thoughts, words and actions are governed by pure love. The temptations of the sanctified,—for they are often most fiercely assailed,—are of external origin. A skillful general desires most the destruction of those forces that can harm him most. Satan is an able and artful warrior. He lays his deepest plots, and exerts his mightiest energies for the overthrow of those who are seeking to follow the Lord fully, knowing that through them his kingdom suffers its greatest losses. If any one in probation supposes himself beyond the reach of temptations, he is either already within the grasp of Satan, or he is most wofully deceived. But he whose "life is hid with Christ in God," feels secure, though Satan rages. The merely justified has to meet, not only the onsets of Satan, but is compelled to struggle against the remaining corruptions of his own heart. The one has both a civil and foreign war to carry on at once; the other has a foreign war alone. Beloved, hasten to the fountain that is opened for sin and uncleanness. This is the will of God, even your sanctification. Give yourself no rest until you know and feel that the blood of Jesus cleanses you from all sin.

Holiness, Entire Sanctification and Perfect Love are different Bible terms used to denote essentially the same state of grace. The same building may be called a house, a residence or a home. Each has its different shade of meaning. But whatever term is used to designate a state of conformity to the will of God, it must not be lost sight of for a single moment, that love constitutes an important element. Christ says, "Love your enemies, bless them that curse you, do good to them that hate you, and pray for them that despitefully use you and persecute you; that ye may be the children of your Father which is in heaven."—Matt. 5: 44, 45. If one professes to be wholly sanctified to God, and manifests continually towards those who do not indorse him a malignant spirit that loses no opportunity to wound them with tongue or pen, we must not receive his profession. Weighed in the balance of God's sanctuary he is found wanting.

But Perfect Love never gives its countenance to sin in any shape or guise. It loves the sinner, but it hates sin. It reproves it whenever found. It is not spared because it is fashionable or profitable. True holiness is not wanting in any of its parts. It does not "tithe mint and anise and cummin," and neglect weightier matters.

CHAPTER XXXII.

PERFECTION.

THERE is no prejudice against the use of the word perfection in connection with human affairs generally. Who objects to a tailor who makes a perfect fit for his customers? If, in a piece of cloth purchased, an imperfection is found, it is promptly returned; if, in a tool a flaw is discovered, it is replaced by a better one. The doctor does not suffer in reputation by effecting perfect cures; nor does the lawyer in making for his client a perfect defence. Why should any who claim to be Christians be intolerant of the use of the word perfection in connection with Christian character? Why should they deem it almost blasphemy for one who was on the point of spiritual death, to affirm that Christ has affected for him a perfect cure?

Instead of the Scriptures forbidding us to be perfect, as might be inferred from the teachings of some ministers and churches, they expressly command it.

"Be ye therefore perfect, even as your Father which is in heaven is perfect."—Matt. 5:48. The phrase "even as your Father which is in heaven is perfect," does not denote the *degree* to which we are to be perfect, but *the reason* why we should be perfect. Be perfect servants of a perfect God.

"I am the Almighty God: walk before me and be thou perfect."—Gen. 17:1.

The Apostle Paul tells us that his object in preaching Christ was, not to encourage men to believe that if they called themselves Christians they would of necessity be saved, not to build up a society but to produce in each of these a perfect Christian character. "Whom we preach, warning every man, and teaching every man in all wisdom: that we may present every man perfect in Christ Jesus."—Col. 1:28.

For this same purpose the truths of the Bible were revealed to man. "All Scripture is given by inspiration of God, and is profitable for doctrine, for reproof, for correction, for instruction in righteousness that the man of God may be perfect, thoroughly furnished unto all good works."—II Tim. 3:16, 17.

What shall we do with these plain passages of the Word of God? Of course they can be explained away to the satisfaction of worldlings and cavilers in the churches. So can any other texts that teach doctrines, or enjoin prohibitions or precepts repugnant to the sensual, worldly spirit of the age. This is done to a fearful extent. The cross is wreathed with flowers, and instead of being the symbol of the maligned, despised, persecuted religion of the man of Nazareth, it has become the symbol of baptized worldliness and a refined sensualism and fashionable sentimentality. The religion which takes the Bible for its basis, but claims the right to eliminate from its teachings whatever is distasteful to the "culture" of the day, is not the Christianity of the New Testament. It may adopt its forms, use its language and claim to be its representative, but it is all a delusion and a sham. There is not in it the one essential of true religion —submission to God. Stress is laid upon what it is fashionable to observe.

We have no right to reject the words of the Bible or the ideas which they represent and still claim to be Christians.

The word "perfect" is, then, a New Testament term with a well defined meaning. We must accept the word in its Scripture meaning, and neither reject it nor explain it away.

The command "be perfect," does not express any well known, definite act like the command "repent;" nor any particular experience like being "born again." It is taken in a wider sense; with a greater latitude of meaning. It applies to a child of God in various stages of his experience. A blade of corn may be said to be perfect in a dozen different stages of its growth.

But if, before it was ripe, it stopped growing, it would not be perfect. So, at a certain period of his experience, a person may be said to be a perfect Christian, and yet his attainments in piety be small in comparison with what they are after years of toil and sorrow.

A young man leaves the district school for the academy. He has studied hard and begins to reap some of its fruits. The teacher, proud of his pupil, says: "He is perfect in his mathematics. He can solve every problem in the hardest arithmetic." After three years in the academy with a lesson every day in mathematics, he is sent to college, recommended as "perfect in mathematics." He is well versed in algebra, geometry and trigonometry. After studying mathematics in college four years, having completed his course, he graduates with the highest honors of the mathematical department. He then goes to some special school and spends perhaps three years more in studying mathematics as applied to astronomy or to civil engineering. Then again he is pronounced perfect in his well-mastered study. At the close of a life of unremitting study, we hear him say with the immortal Sir Isaac Newton, "I seem like a child standing upon the shore of the ocean gathering pebbles. I have picked up here and there a pearl, while the great ocean of truth lies unexplored before me." So when one becomes a Christian his conversion may be perfect; when his heart is purified by faith he may be perfectly sanctified; and still after years of growth in grace we hear him saying with Job when he got a sight of God, "Wherefore I abhor myself and repent in dust and ashes." Yet God had twice pronounced him perfect.

Hence the Apostle says of himself, "Not as though I had already attained, either were already perfect."—Phil. 3:12. Yet almost in the same breath he says, "Let us therefore as many as be perfect." This implies that he counted himself among those that are perfect.

We never read in the Bible of any being made perfect by faith. We read of persons being "justified by faith."—Rom. 9:30; Rom. 5:1; Gal. 3:24: "sanctified by faith."—Acts 15:9; Acts 26:18; but never once a person being made perfect by faith. Quite another element enters into the making of the saints perfect. "For it became him, for whom are all things, and by whom are all things, in bringing many sons unto glory, to make the captain of their salvation perfect through sufferings."— Heb. 2:10. The perfection which the Gospel enjoins upon the saints can only be attained by fidelity in doing and patience in suffering all the will of God. A symmetrical, well-balanced, unswerving Christian character is not obtained at once. When Paul and Barnabas would "confirm the souls of the disciples," they did it by "exhorting them to continue in the faith, and that we must through much tribulation enter into the kingdom of God."—Acts 14:22.

We must not confound the perfection which the Gospel requires with perfect love or entire sanctification. The Scriptures do not use these terms as synonymous.

We are not to seek Christian perfection so much by praying for it as a blessing to be received in an instant by faith. as by "patient continuance in well-doing." We are to seek it as a well disposed boy seeks a vigorous manhood by shunning the vices and overcoming the temptations to which he is exposed, and by doing faithfully the duties to which he is called.

We must not conclude that we shall by any natural process grow out of our imperfections and become perfect Christians, without any special effort in that direction. Grace, in every stage and in every degree, is from God. The prayer of Peter for the saints is, "But the God of all grace, who hath called us unto his eternal glory by Christ Jesus, after that ye have suffered awhile, make you perfect, stablish, strengthen, settle you."—I Pet. 5:10.

The Apostle gives a good example of the way to profess perfection: "Not as though I had already attained, either were already perfect: but I follow after, if that I may apprehend that for which also I am apprehended of Christ Jesus. Brethren, I count not myself to have apprehended: but this one thing *I do*, forgetting those things which are behind, and reaching forth unto those things which are before, I press toward the mark for the prize of the high calling of God in Christ Jesus. Let us therefore, as many as be perfect, be thus minded."—Phil. 3:12-15.

The Bible teaches us that we are to render a perfect service to God. Nothing short of this will meet our obligations. "Be ye therefore perfect, even as your Father which is in heaven is perfect."—Matt. 5:48. This is a plain command. But many err in supposing that this perfection is one of knowledge or of judgment. It is no such thing. In this sense God only is perfect. The perfection which God requires is a perfection of love.

In many things we are necessarily imperfect, and always shall be. But, by the grace of God, we may become perfect in love. Our capacity for this kind of perfection does not depend upon our talents or our circumstances. He who has but one dollar can give all the money he has, just as well as he who has a million. I can love God with all *my* heart; an angel can love God no more than with all *his* heart. The requirements of God are reasonable. They cover only what we are, or what we are capable, by His help, of becoming. Whatever our defects, we may have the "love of God shed abroad in our hearts by the Holy Ghost given unto us."—Rom. 5:5. When this is the case—when we love God with all the heart, mind and strength, and our neighbor as ourselves—then have we perfect love. Not that it is incapable of increase. As our capacities enlarge, our love will increase, but as we now are we can do no better; and it is accepted according to what a man hath, and not according to what he hath not.

If we have this perfect love to God, it will be manifested—not in words only, but in actions.

We shall keep His commandments. Our study will be to know His will, with an honest intention of doing it, with whatever losses or crosses it may be attended. We shall ask, What does God require?—not what is pleasing to self or popular with the world.

We shall manifest our love to God, by acts of kindness, just as far as we have the opportunity, to all of His creatures. We shall take the greatest delight in those who love Him most. "If a man say, I love God, and hateth his brother, he is a liar; for he that loveth not his brother whom he hath seen, how can he love God whom he hath not seen?"—I John 4:20. This is emphatic. It shows that our professions of love to God amount to absolutely nothing, unless we love our fellow-men especially those who are striving to keep His commandments. The charity that Paul speaks of in the thirteenth chapter of first Corinthians, without which the strongest faith and the largest faith and the largest gifts, and even martyrdom for the truth, will profit us nothing, manifests itself in tender feelings and kind conduct towards our fellow-men.

Do not profess perfect love, if you are cross, unamiable, and unkind at home. If you have not natural affection, you certainly have not supernatural. If you do not do as well as the brutes, do not profess to be like the angels of God. If you are not kind to her whom you have sworn to cherish, or to those whose protector nature has constituted you, stop your professions at once. You have already sins enough to sink you to hell, without adding hypocrisy to them.

If you cannot treat your brother, whose opinion may not always coincide with yours, as civilly as men of the world treat each other, do not profess perfect love. It does not require any grace to love those who agree with our opinions, and who yield in willing deference to our authority. Common sinners do as well as that.

If you are injuring your brother's influence by unkind words and injurious insinuations, do not profess perfect love. Remember that "Love worketh no ill to his neighbor."—Rom. 13:10. Therefore if you are doing him harm by talking against him when at the same time you say that you love him, you show that at the best, you are self-deceived. You are mistaken in your profession. You do not enjoy that state of grace that you think you do. A little candid reflection would convince you of this. There is always a care for the reputation of those that we tenderly love. "If we love one another, God dwelleth in us, and his love is perfected in us."—I John 4:12.

CHAPTER XXXIII.

DEAD TO SIN.

THAT many who profess the blessing of entire sanctification are greatly lacking in some of its essential elements is painfully evident. They are not "blameless and harmless, the sons of God without rebuke." They do not "shine as lights in the world." Not that one can reach on earth such a state that those who are disposed to find fault with him can not do it. This is impossible. Our Saviour was perpetually found fault with by the most noted religionists of His day, and at last put to death by them. But we may get where we have the constant approbation of God;—where we please Him in all that we do, and in all that we say. Our lives may be in harmony with His word taken in its plain, evident meaning.

1. Some have not the courage to bear a faithful testimony for God and His truth. They speak against sin in the general, but they are careful not to attack, in a determined manner, popular sins. They pass them over in a way not calculated to attract attention. Where it is fash-

ionable for professing Christians to dress like the world they have nothing to say against it. If the preacher's salary is raised by renting the pews, they let it pass in silence, though the Bible plainly forbids it. If men prominent in the Church belong to secret, oath-bound societies they do not try to convince them that this stands in the way of their salvation. In short, they shun to declare the whole counsel of God. They tell many truths. But they are not thorough. The work they do is superficial. If they are themselves saved at last, it will be, as by fire.

2. Some evidently have not the love that is essential to salvation. They abuse, in no stinted manner, those who do not give them the indorsement they want. When things go contrary they behave very much as men of the world do when they are downright mad; yet they insist upon it that their bitter denunciations and personal invectives are prompted by love. They seem to forget that "love worketh no ill to his neighbor." Towards those who favor them, but give no other evidence of superior piety, they are kind and complaisant.

3. Others are self-willed. They seem consecrated, but it appears to be to have their own way. They make it a point of conscience to have every one come to their terms and submit to their conditions. They are bold and courageous, in defense of their own opinions and actions.

They make the way to heaven so narrow that it seems almost impossible for any one to travel in it. After getting those who oppose them out of the church, if they can, they generally end with either joining the formal, fashionable church which they have specially denounced; or they become a sect in themselves.

The trouble in these and similar cases is, there is an effort to get that sanctified to God, which is not capable of being thoroughly and permanently sanctified—the old nature. The Apostle says: "Put off . . . the old man which is corrupt according to the deceitful lusts."—Eph. 4:22. The modern interpretation is, "Sanctify him." So he makes an effort to get sanctified, and professes that it is done. But he will not stay sanctified. It is like putting a thin coating of silver on an iron spoon. A little wear brings the base material to the surface. A few knocks, and the old nature is apparent. The coating here and there comes off and he presents the appearance of being sanctified in spots.

There is an experience which will enable us to stand true to God, and true to our own convictions everywhere. Job had it. Paul lived in this state till death. God's true saints have had it in all ages. Paul tells us in his own experience how it is obtained. "I am crucified with Christ, nevertheless I live; yet not I, but Christ liveth in me."—Gal. 2:20.

Crucifixion was a lingering death. It was not sudden, like decapitation. The victim might linger in agony for days. So, one does not die out to the world all at once. The struggle between the life of self and death to self, the world, and sin may go on for a long time. But the sooner it is ended the better. The sudden piercing of the spear, though it may look cruel, is really an act of mercy. Anything that keeps the old nature alive but protracts the misery and postpones the triumph. For after death cometh the resurrection life.

Crucifixion was a death inflicted by others. The victim was simply passive. Others nailed him to the cross—others planted the cross in its place.

Many fail to go forward in their experience because they lose sight of this truth. They do not accept the ill treatment that they receive because of their fidelity to Christ, as a part of their necessary discipline. They blame those who inflict it. Resentment takes the place of submission. They give blow for blow. When reviled they pay it back as best they can. If led to the slaughter they make desperate and successful efforts to escape. They will not consent to be nailed to the cross. Their whole life is a life of self. They may be very zealous, but it is the zeal of Jehu and not of Paul. They spare no pains to herald their devotion to Christ. "Come and see my zeal for the Lord of hosts." They may be exceedingly plain and outspoken, and uncompromising; but they are simply acting out their natural disposition, modified and restrained somewhat by grace. It is a great opportunity for growing in grace and becoming strong for God that we miss, when we refuse to suffer patiently the wrongs inflicted upon us, it may be, by those who ought to stand by us. Diamonds are found in beds of gravel. The worthless clay becomes fitted for the walls of a palace by becoming moulded into shape and passing through the fire. The passionate, the proud, the self-willed, the worldly, may be fitted for a heaven of purity by consenting to die unto sin and unto the world. All they have to do is, to get and to keep the consent of their wills; the cross will be duly prepared. Let them quietly submit, the work will be done. More submission would make greater saints. We fail to get a solid experience because we will not hold still and suffer the crucifixion to go on and become completed. We do not reap the result desired because we will not accept the process. Our claim to having faith in God is worthless, so long as we refuse to have confidence in His mode of working. Faith in God is faith in His providence as well as in His word. It believes in what He does, as well as in what He says. Job saw the hand of God in making him poor, as well as in making him rich. "The Lord gave; and the Lord hath taken away: blessed be the name of the Lord."—Job 1:21. He blessed the Lord in his affliction, and the Lord blessed him out of his affliction. His latter state was better than his first.

The only way to life is through the valley of the shadow of death. The worm weaves its shroud to get its wings. It dies to the earth that it may live in the air. After the crucifixion of self comes the resurrection to life. As the old nature dies we are transformed into the divine nature. The change is real, and may be permanent. The whole being is changed. The intellect is stronger and more active. Truth is comprehended and retained more easily than before. The conscience is corrected, and invested with sovereign authority over the entire man. Truth is loved and sought after and embraced. There is a keen sensitiveness to right and wrong. The side of right may have but few adherents, and they despised; but it can never be so unpopular that it is not, when seen, espoused and defended.

The bodily appetites undergo a great transformation. Those that are unnatural are removed. Those that are natural and right within proper limits are subdued and brought into subjection to reason and conscience. The reins of government have passed from the carnal to the spiritual. He is still in the body, but not in the flesh.

The flesh no longer dominates and controls. A blessed harmony prevails throughout his entire being. One thus saved is no longer at war with himself. The rebel is dead. The *I* that made trouble is crucified. It no longer lives. Christ has taken possession. He sits upon the throne of the affections. The words and actions prompted by His Spirit are in harmony with His teachings, "It is a faithful saying: for if we be dead with him, we shall also live with him: If we suffer, we shall also reign with him: if we deny him he also will deny us."—II Tim. 2:11, 12.

CHAPTER XXXIV.

ROOTS OF BITTERNESS.

IT is a great thing to get saved;—it is much greater to keep saved. Many lose communion with God by compromising with sin—many more by losing their love and becoming harsh and uncharitable. In the same breath in which we are commanded to "follow holiness without which no man shall see the Lord" we are charged to look "diligently, lest any root of bitterness springing up trouble you, and thereby many be defiled."—Heb. 12:15.

These "roots of bitterness" are troublesome things. What trouble they make in the Conference, and in the Church, especially if there is a strong, leading spirit nourished by the root! There is almost no end to the mischief it can make. It brings in a spirit of division, it instigates to church trials, it stirs up a hasty spirit; it breaks up societies and ruins souls. As alcohol, the bane of our race, is extracted from grain from which the bread of our race is made, so this "root of bitterness" is a perversion of holiness without which no one can be saved. To *discern it* one must *look diligently*. Much that passes for the fruit of holiness grows upon this root of bitterness. It produces many sermons, and exhortations, and articles for the papers which claim to be inspired by the Holy Spirit. From knowing that what goes into a building is suitable for food you cannot decide that what comes out is good to nourish human beings. The grain may come out flour for bread; or it may come out liquid hell-fire. It depends upon whether there is a mill or a still inside. So what one gets out of a text depends upon what there is in the heart. If there is love, the severest words will be seasoned with tenderness. They may be sharper than a two-edged sword; but, to the honest soul that is wounded, there comes the oil of joy for mourning.

But if, instead of love within there is the root of bitterness the words will drive rather than draw; the arrow may be well aimed; but it will leave a poisoned wound which refuses to be healed. Those who come under the influence of this root of bitterness become less kind, less amiable, than they were before they professed holiness. Those who live in love may stir up enmity, but their enemies are drawn to them in spite of themselves.

It is not enough that we are zealous, and our zeal is successful in making converts. What is the character of our converts? Are they filled with that love of God which leads them to keep His commandments? "For this is the love of

God that we keep his commandments: and his commandments are not grievous."—I John 5:3. Or, on the contrary, are they conformed to this world? If not, if they are simple and plain, are they bitter in their spirit and denunciatory in their tone?

Christ said of the Pharisees, "Ye compass sea and land to make one proselyte, and when he is made, ye make him two-fold more the child of hell than yourselves."—Matt. 23:15. We must see to it that we are not of that sort, and that our converts are not of that sort. Zeal and success in making converts and in getting them into the church are not evidence that those who have the zeal and meet with the success are children of God. Both those who lead and those who follow may be blind. The church and the world greatly need those who can and will do true work for God. Many who seem willing to do it are not in a spiritual condition to do it. They are either too complaisant or too bitter. Their converts are either baptized worldlings or self-complacent bigots.

Who will have true charity and will do faithful work for God?

CHAPTER XXXV.

BE YE HOLY.

NO matter how brilliant a beginning one may make in the divine life, if he does not learn to act from a sense of his obligations to God, his religious career will, in all probability be a short one. A road all the way down hill is not generally long. Good impulses are often of only short duration. When Lord Nelson, the greatest of England's naval heroes, opened battle upon the combined fleet of France and Spain, a fleet nearly double the size of his own, he nailed at his mast head the signal, "England expects every man to do his duty." If veterans in the excitement of battle need the inspiration which a sense of duty only can impart, much more do Christians in the conflicts which come upon them in the midst of depression and discouragement. Our course, as followers of Jesus, should be determined by what we *ought* to do, and not by what we *feel* like doing. We must, then, pay the highest respect to the commands of God. Let us consider one of these commands. "But as he which hath called you is holy. so be ye holy in all manner of conversation."—I Pet. 1:15. This is not an isolated command. It is found in varied forms in every portion of the Bible. It stands out prominently in every dispensation. Some of the early patriarchs furnish bright examples of obedience to its requirements. "Enoch walked with God" so closely that he was taken up bodily to the abode of the blessed without ever tasting death. Job demonstrated to the world that it is possible for a man to keep holiness, though he loses everything else. Daniel proved that a man can live a holy life in the courts of kings, surrounded by every temptation that pleasure and ambition can furnish. No command of the Bible is stated more clearly, and few more frequently, than the requirement to be holy.

It is an *important* command. Viewed in whatever light it may be, it is one of the most weighty of all the requirements which God has made of man. Obedience to it is crowned with the greatest blessings God can bestow, disobedience to it makes the transgressor wretched for time and for eternity.

You who have been accustomed to look upon holiness as simply a privilege which can be neglected with impunity, be convinced of your mistake. If you neglect it, you neglect it at no less a peril than the loss of Heaven. "And there shall in no wise enter into it anything that defileth, neither whatsoever worketh abomination, or maketh a lie: but they which are written in the Lamb's book of life."—Rev. 21:27. "Follow peace with all men, and holiness, without which no man shall see the Lord."—Heb. 12:14.

These are plain statements. The whole Bible is in harmony with them. No contradictory teaching can be found between its hallowed pages.

Let us examine briefly a few of the features of this command.

1. *It requires a holy nature.* It calls upon us *to be holy.* It demands nothing less than a complete renovation of our moral natures. For this, the Gospel has made the most ample provision. The avowed object of Christ's coming was that, "We, being delivered out of the hand of our enemies, might serve him without fear, in holiness and righteousness before him all the days of our life."—Luke 1:74, 75. Our sins are our greatest and most dangerous enemies. The angel who announced the coming of Christ said, "Thou shalt call his name JESUS: for he shall save his people from their sins."—Matt. 1:21. Then ask the Lord, for Christ's sake, to save you from all your sins, and make you holy. All admit that He can save from the greater and grosser sins— from murder and theft and profanity. Why can He not then save from the more subtle and refined sins, from envy and pride and discontent?

What reason is there that He cannot? What text of Scripture is it which goes to prove that Christ cannot save from every sin, to which man is subject, those who obey Him? When God makes a requirement, He gives the ability to meet it. The two go together. He is not a hard master. He does not attempt to reap where He has not sown.

All that is said about the natural weakness and depravity of our natures is true. But the Gospel proposes to make us new creatures. So the bare fact that God commands us to be holy is proof conclusive that He has made ample provision for us to be holy. Exceeding great and precious promises are given, on purpose that we may avail ourselves of them, and thus become "partakers of the divine nature"—that is, become holy. (II Pet. 1:4.)

The command we are considering requires us to be holy in our whole manner of living. Our holiness must be not only experimental but practical. It must manifest itself in all the ordinary affairs of life. The word "conversation" is one of the few words which have changed their meaning since King James' translation of the Bible was made. Then, it meant one's general conduct, or behaviour. Now, we restrict its meaning to familiar discourse with each other by word of mouth. In both senses God requires us to be holy.

Our language must be on all occasions chaste and pure. Here is a general rule for all Christians: "Let no corrupt communication proceed out of your mouth, but that which is good to the use of edifying, that it may minister grace unto the hearers."—Eph. 4:29. A holy heart employs a holy tongue He is deceived who thinks his heart is holy while his conversation is unholy. The state of the heart determines the character of the language. Corrupt communication proceeds from a corrupt heart.

If we are holy in conversation we shall be careful not to say anything to the injury of anyone, unless the law of love requires it, in order to prevent him from injuring others. He that shall dwell in God's holy hill "backbiteth not with his tongue, nor doeth evil to his neighbor, nor taketh up a reproach against his neighbor."— Ps. 15:3. A holiness that does not save from evil speaking is of little worth. As a rule, if you cannot say something good of the absent, then say nothing at all. When tempted to cast some reflections upon those who are not where they can explain what is calculated to lower them in the estimation of others, then resist the temptation and find something good to say of them and you will find a blessing to your soul.

The holiness required must manifest itself in all our business matters. It demands the strictest honesty; but it goes beyond that. Men who borrow money through the influence of representations which they know are not strictly true, should not make any profession of holiness, nor even of justifying grace. A religion devoid of honesty is utterly worthless. No pains should be taken to keep it; for it is not worth keeping. We must exercise a good conscience in every business transaction with which we are connected. The directions which Paul gives to Christian servants, if carried out, would make their services in good demand by all who have need of service. "Servants, be obedient to them that are your masters according to the flesh, with fear and trembling, in singleness of your heart, as unto Christ; not with eye-service, as men-pleasers: but as the servants of Christ, doing the will of God from the heart; with good will doing service, as to the Lord, and not to men. Knowing that whatsoever good thing any man doeth, the same shall he receive of the Lord, whether he be bond or free."—Eph. 6:5-8. There are two remarkable things in this passage. What we do for others conscientiously, those for whom we do it stand to us in the place of Christ. That for service thus rendered God will reward us.

This is the holiness that God requires of us. It must be professed by word of mouth. It must manifest itself in our love for the saints, in our love for the Bible and for communion with God in prayer. It must take on the most thoroughly practical character before the world, and show its influence in the bargains we make, in the fidelity with which we discharge every trust committed to us, in the dress we wear, in the manner in which we walk and talk in our families and in the various relations of life. It will carry an element of sincerity and honesty into the smallest, as well as into the largest transactions of life. "Is this right?" will be a question that will come up repeatedly before the mind; and if the answer is in the negative, no matter what pleasure or profit the proposed action may promise, it goes no farther.

One who is thus holy will be persecuted,—there is no help for that—but he will be respected. "For he that in these things serveth Christ is acceptable to God and approved of men."—Rom. 14:18.

Beloveds, do not say that you cannot be thus holy. If there were not a single promise in the Bible that God would make you holy, the very fact that He commands it, is, in itself, the fullest promise that He will bestow all the grace needed to those who seek it. Then, from this moment begin to seek holiness. Every gain that you make inwardly, manifest it outwardly. Let those around you profit by every blessing that God sends upon your soul. Prove to the world, by leading a holy life, that the doctrine of holiness is true.

No arguments of geologists can raise the price of real estate in any section of country so rapidly as can a well sending up its hundreds of barrels of oil a day. Scripture proofs of the doctrine of holiness cannot convince the people that it is attainable, so unanswerably as a holy life. Then, do not be sinning and repenting any longer. Consecrate your life to Him, not only in general but in the detail. Live wholly for Him. "Be ye holy in all manner of living."

CHAPTER XXXVI.

ARE YOU HOLY?

DO not evade the question. Press it home upon your conscience. Ponder it well. Keep it in your mind until an honest and correct conclusion is reached. You readily admit that there would be reason for uneasiness were you justly in doubt as to whether or not you were converted. The obligation to be converted is no stronger than the obligation to be holy. Both rest on the same foundation—the command of God. This is no less explicit in the one case than in the other. Why should we be born of the Spirit? The ready answer is, Jesus says, "Ye must be born again." Why ought we to be holy? The same Divine Teacher declares, "This is the will of God, even your sanctification." Is the one essential to salvation? The infallible Guide, who says, "Except ye be converted and become as little children, ye can in no case enter into the kingdom of heaven," says also, "Without holiness no man shall see the Lord." If you are indifferent as to your personal sanctity, you have reason to doubt the genuineness of your conversion. Truly regenerated souls aspire after holiness. Even where the system of theology in which they have been educated denies its attainableness, they still long for it as something desirable. With the pious Watts, they exclaim:

> "Could we but climb where Moses stood,
> And view the landscape o'er.
> Not Jordan's stream, nor death's cold flood,
> Could fright us from that shore."

This is the language of a converted soul. "Could we but climb," how gladly would we do it. Were we satisfied that it is within the reach of possibility, we would make a desperate effort. Well, earnest Christian, you may ascend, even here, to Pisgah's summit. You may dwell in the land of Beulah, where the sun always shines. Holiness is possible. Consider. Would you impose upon your tender child of ten years of age, a load which would require the utmost strength of a full grown man to carry? Would you require your son, so far recovered from a protracted sickness, as to be able to sit up an hour at a time, to do a day's work that none but an able-bodied man could accomplish? "If ye then being evil," would not require impossibilities, how much less would "your Father in heaven?" God commands us, "Be ye holy." Pharaoh may demand the full tale of brick without furnishing material; but God never imposes a duty without providing every needed help for its fulfilment. Were we obliged to obtain a holy heart by our own efforts, we might despair. If we were "to grow up" into holiness by habits of obedience, discouragement might take place. But a holy heart is as much the work of God as a conversion. The Word says, "If we confess our sins, he is faithful and just to forgive us our sins, and to cleanse us from all unrighteousness." —I John 1:9. Who forgives sin? God only. Who cleanses us from all unrighteousness? The same Almighty Being. None, then, need despair. Do not limit the Holy One of Israel. If you meet the conditions, God will make even you holy. If holiness be God's work, try ever so long and earnestly, and you cannot grow up into it. Ask Him now to "sprinkle clean water upon you, and ye shall be clean;" to put His Spirit within you, and to cause you to walk in His statutes. As Dr. Adam Clarke says: "In no part of the Scriptures are we directed to seek holiness *gradatim* (that is, step by step, gradually). We are to come to God as well for an instantaneous and complete purification from all sin as for an instantaneous pardon. Neither the *seriatim* pardon nor the *gradatim* purification exists in the Bible. It is when the soul is purified from all sin that it can properly grow in grace, and in the knowledge of our Lord Jesus Christ! As the field may be expected to produce a good crop, and all the seed vegetate, when the thorns, thistles, and briars, and noxious weeds of every kind are grubbed out of it. Come to God, then, in faith to make you holy; and soon exulting, you will sing:

> "Rejoicing now in earnest hope
> I stand, and from the mountain top
> See all the land below."

CHAPTER XXXVII.

THE CARNAL MIND.

WHEN our Saviour was teaching Nicodemus the nature of the new birth, the latter inquired: "How can these things be?" The Saviour did not attempt to explain *the how*. He insisted upon the *fact*, He made no effort to remove the mystery of the *manner*. To endeavor to do it would be as unsatisfactory as to try to show where the wind comes from and where it goes to. Those who receive it must receive it by faith. "Verily, verily, I say unto thee, we speak that we do know, and testify that we have seen; and ye receive not our witness."—John 3:11. Those who know least about *how* food builds up the body, often have the keenest appetites, and the best blood. So those who are least inquisitive about the *manner* in which the Holy Spirit operates upon the mind to sanctify it, often have the greatest degree of the Spirit's influence upon their hearts. He who receives the kingdom of God receives it, not as a philosopher after all his questions have been answered and his doubts removed, but as a little child, who takes it on trust, and asks no questions. "Verily I say unto you, Whosoever shall not receive the kingdom of God as a little child shall in no wise enter therein."—Luke 18:17.

Speculations in religious things easily become perplexing and unprofitable. Those who make a hobby of talking and writing about the "carnal mind" are in danger of running to an extreme that is not Scriptural.

There are seven different Greek words which, in the New Testament, are translated "mind."

1. γνώμη,—purpose, judgment. "But without thy *mind* would I do nothing."—Philemon, 14. "These have one *mind*."—Rev. 17:13. "He purposed [literally it was his purpose] to return."—Acts. 20:3. "Yet I give my *judgment*." —I Cor. 7:25, etc.

2. ἔννοια, inner purpose. "Arm yourselves likewise with the same *mind*."—I Pet. 4:1.

3. νους, mind, understanding. "God gave them over to a reprobate *mind*."—Rom. 1:28. "But I see another law in my members, warring against the law of my *mind*."—Rom. 7:23. "Then opened he their *understanding*."—Luke 24:45. "I will pray with the *understanding* also."—I Cor. 14:15.

4. ψυχη,—soul, affections. "Made their *minds* evil affected."—Acts 14.2. "With one *mind* striving together."—Philippians 1:27. "Take no thought for your *life*."—Matt. 6:25. "But are not able to kill the *soul*."—Matt. 10:28.

THE CARNAL MIND. 241

5. νόημα,—mind, thought. "Their *minds* were blinded."—II Cor. 3:14. "Shall keep your hearts and *minds*."—Phil. 4:7. "We are not ignorant of his *devices*."—II Cor. 2:11. "Bringing into captivity every *thought*."—II Cor. 10:5.

6. διάνοια, mind, intellect. "*With* all thy soul, and with all thy *mind*."—Matt. 22:37. "I will put my laws into their *mind*."—Heb. 8:10. "Having the *understanding* darkened."—Eph. 4:18. "Hath given us an *understanding*."—I John 5:20.

7. Φρονημα,—mind, inclination. "Because the carnal *mind* is enmity against God."—Rom. 8:7. "Knoweth what (is) the *mind* of the Spirit."—Rom. 8.27. "To be carnally *minded* is death; but to be spiritually *minded* is life and peace."—Rom. 8:6.

These are all the passages in which the last word is found in the New Testament. It means "what one has in mind, what one thinks, feels, wills."

A man has but one mind, one intellect, one soul. He may have many thoughts, inclinations and purposes. If he is in his natural state, unrenewed by the grace of God, his mind taken up with worldly thoughts, and plans, and purposes, he is *carnally minded*,—in a state of spiritual death. If he has been truly converted to God, his mind is taken up with spiritual things. Whatevever may engage his attention for the time, God is never lost sight of in all his plans and purposes. The bent of his mind is toward God. He is "not in the flesh, but in the Spirit," for "the Spirit of God dwells in him." But if, while he is devoted to Christ on the whole, he, at the same time, is partisan in his spirit, and attaches himself to some leading man, so as to follow his dictation, he is in a measure carnal, though still a babe in Christ. "And I, brethren, could not speak unto you as unto spiritual, but as unto carnal, even as unto babes in Christ." "For ye are yet carnal; for whereas there is among you envying, and strife, and divisions, are ye not carnal, and walk as men?"—I Cor. 3:1, 3. But as they were not wholly given up to this spirit of strife and division, they had not yet reached the state of being *carnally minded*—that is, a state of death, though they were on their way to it.

If one is *sanctified wholly*, his mind, his will, is so changed that earthly things lose their attractions, and he sets his affections on things above, and not on things on the earth. Such persons follow the Lord fully. But their minds are not destroyed. The "carnal mind" is never so destroyed as to do away with the freedom of the will. There is need to constantly watch and pray. Things that may be lawful in themselves may be easily run to sinful excess. The love that begins in the Spirit may end in the flesh.

Eating "their meat with gladness" may degenerate into a desire for luxuries. "Diligence in business" may easily run into a love of the world. Even a fixed determination "to follow the Lord fully" may unconsciously slide into a consecration to one's own will, so that those will be fellowshipped who indorse us and our methods, and those who do not will be unchristianized.

The Sun of Righteousness may shine with cloudless splendor into our souls; but we must keep the soul constantly open to its influences. We cannot lay up in one hour a stock of light and heat for the next. We may in faith pray, "Give us this day our daily bread;" but we shall need to pray the same prayer to-morrow. Our dependence upon God is absolute and unremitting. As the law of gravity draws the earth toward the sun every moment, so does the law of love draw a saved soul toward God.

CHAPTER XXXVIII.

SEEKING HOLINESS.

THE way to seek holiness is, *to seek it*. You must be *determined* about it. You never put in any "ifs" when you are looking for something which you *know* can be found. So, when seeking for holiness do not say, even to yourself, "I will have it, *if it is for me.*" Such an expression will weaken your faith. You know it is for you. Leave the "if" out. God commands you to be holy. That is evidence enough. You have not as strong an evidence that you can gain anything else for which you seek. God requires that you should serve Him in the beauty of holiness. This service is reasonable, because it is within your reach. The servants of some masters are required to furnish their own livery. It is not so with the servants of Christ. When He says, "Put on thy beautiful garments" (Isa. 52:1), He has them at hand, all fitted and furnished. His supply never fails. He requires no pay. All He asks of you is to put them on. But in doing this you must follow His directions.

Do not expect God to do what He commands

you to do. He will help you, but you must help yourself. No amount of praying will take the place of obedience. Many pray for cleansing, to whom God says, "Cleanse yourselves."—James 4:8; II Cor. 7:1.

In putting on new clothes you put off the old ones. This is the order of nature. It is the order of God. It is of no use to try to reverse this order. If you attempt it you will fail. And you will fail just as often as you attempt it.

If you want God to save you from filthy appetites, you must cease from filthy practices. If you would have Him to take away the love of tobacco, you must forever quit using tobacco. You ask the Lord to take all the pride out of your heart; He commands you to lay all the evidences of it off from your person. Until you consent to do it, you cannot go a step farther. Do not let time-serving teachers deceive you on this point. They may tell you that God does not care about dress. He does care about the dress of His children; or He would not have said so much respecting it, in His word. In short you cannot take one step forward in the divine life, without some outward reformation of manners.

We once asked a Roman Catholic sister, devoted to the cause of education, what her work was. She replied, "Sometimes I am preceptress fo a Young Ladies' Seminary; and sometimes I am janitress, having to close the doors and sweep the halls; but I am as ready for the one as for the other."

So, if you would have *true holiness* you must set yourself apart to do whatever God requires at your hands.

In seeking holiness come to God for yourself. Realize that it is a transaction wholly between God and your own soul. It may do good to get others to pray for you. It will do no harm, unless you depend on their prayers. But you must come to God for yourself. Make your supplication to Him. Believe that He hears. You are asking what He has promised—therefore expect it. "And this is the confidence that we have in him, that, if we ask anything according to his will, he heareth us. And if we know that he hear us, whatsoever we ask, we know that we have the petitions that we desired of him.— I John 5:14, 15.

Then when you ask and receive, believe that you receive what you ask for and not some worthless imitation. Your confidence in God can never be misplaced. He will not send you from the throne of grace deceived. Have faith in God.

God has commanded it. Does He say "Thou shalt not steal?" With equal plainness He says, "Be ye holy." (Lev. 20:7. Num. 15:40. I Pet. 1:15, 16.) Here is a plain command, reiterated at long intervals, and under different dispensations. It is not a matter which is left to our own choice. It is imperatively required by our God.

It is necessary to our well being in time and in eternity that we obey this command for: "Without holiness no man shall see the Lord."—Heb. 12:14. How shall we seek holiness? Permit us to answer in the words of C. Larew, written a quarter of a century ago.

"First of all, you will dedicate all to Him. Not but what all you have is His, and has been from the beginning, but you have not so regarded it. You have taken your portion and gone your way heretofore, wasting your Father's gifts in selfish living. Let all this cease at once; and let it be your language, the language of your heart, 'What wilt Thou have me to do?' In a word, consecrate all to your Heavenly Father. How will you do this? We answer,—consent and decide, that all, whether act, word, thought, desire or possessions shall be not as self, or men may will, but as God wills. This, you say, I have tried to do again and again. Doubtless you have, and done it acceptably, too. But here you halted; *you did not believe.* Believe what? you ask. I answer,—the word of God to you at that point. That word is that He 'accepted' and 'received' you. Hear Him,—'Be ye *separate* and I will *receive* you.' You separated yourself, 'presented yourself a living sacrifice;' but *did not believe* on the assurance of His word, that you were accepted. No, you waited for some sign, some sensible manifestation, to come up in your feelings, to assure you that all was received, thus making some preconceived emotion the ground of faith. God does not say, faith cometh by feeling, joyous, peaceful, or otherwise, else you would be right in expecting it to rise and inspire you with faith. Nay, 'FAITH COMETH BY HEARING, and hearing by the word of God.' Therefore, when you consecrate all, as well as you are enabled, you have God's word for the fact that He 'RECEIVES YOU.' This faith will inspire you with feelings of peace, gladness, and great quiet of soul. In God's order, faith gives rise to feelings, and not feelings to faith, as you have erroneously supposed. Hence, you may take God's word and rest upon that. There is no error in this. It is the only way of success; as has been tried and proved by hundreds, after having struggled and floundered in this same error.

"To illustrate: suppose the Lord had said, in His abiding word, 'If any man will place twelve stones upon the earth, and put a lamb thereon, and burn it to ashes, I will receive him, and be a Father unto him, and he shall be my son.' Now, I ask, if you should do this, and the lamb be consumed to ashes, would you not have God's word for your assurance? Yea, as convincingly as if heard audibly from Heaven,—that He 'received you.'

"The Lord has not said this; but He has said, as shown above, that if we 'come out from among them, and BE SEPARATE, and touch not the unclean thing, He WILL RECEIVE US.' Now, I ask, if we thus do, have we not the testimony of the Spirit, written in the word, that we are accepted? Do not fall into the common error of separating the letter of the word from the spirit of the word. You must by faith, regard the letter as the testimony and expression of the mind and spirit of God to you; just as you believe the letter of a friend to be the expression of his mind and spirit. It is through this written word, directly or indirectly, that the Spirit speaks, testifies, or witnesses to us. To regard the word as a dead letter, is to remain in darkness and unbelief. To faith, 'these words are spirit and they are life.' Let us, therefore, '*believe, nothing doubting.*'

"But, says one, 'How am I to know that the consecration is complete!' I answer, if you see nothing to the contrary, it is; for the Lord has said, 'If in anything ye be otherwise minded, God shall reveal even this unto you.' The question is not, what will come up in the future to sacrifice and to suffer. In this, 'Take no thought for the morrow,' applies as well as in anything else. But do you not accept of the will of God as it is made to appear at the present moment? If this is so, this is all that the King requires. Only let this continue, moment by moment, and all will continue acceptable to Him. How great the rest of soul gained by him who thus comes into the truth.

"But, you ask, into what state, or degree of godliness may I now apprehend the Lord has brought me? Are my inward foes all dead? Shall I feel the roots of sin no more from this time?

"This is an important question—one, the understanding of which, may have much to do with your future peace and success in the way of holiness. Many, who have dedicated all, and believed, have been disappointed in finding, after a little while, the old self-nature stir within them, and either took it as an evidence that they were deceived, or soothingly called it 'only temptation;' and have continued to try to believe that all was entirely pure within.

"We forget that there are two parts, or elements, in entire sanctification. The one is the placing of the creature, or sacrifice, upon the altar,—Consecration. The other is the consuming of it to ashes, or to its primitive elements, by God's own fire. The gold must first be put into the crucible; and then melted, and purified, by separating all its inner dross.

"We must first consent and covenant to give

up 'all things,' and then suffer the loss of all. First be nailed to the cross and then 'die daily,' till 'the world is crucified to us,' and 'we live not, but Christ in us.'

"With the first, you have now complied, I trust. If so, you are 'sanctified,' but perhaps not 'wholly;' you are 'holy,' but perhaps not yet 'perfected.' You are now as the gold in the crucible, and can begin to say, 'though he slay me yet will I trust in him;' and hence ready to 'abide the fire.' 'Abide his coming,' as a refiner and purifier. If so, you are fully in the hands of the 'potter,' and He can now begin to mould you as He will, for you will now be able to 'abide,' and not 'draw back,' as you once did when trial came, erroneously considering it an evidence that God was displeased, and no longer accepted you.

"We often make a joyous and gladsome state of the mind, the *only evidence* of our acceptance with the Father. This is a very mischievous error. To do this, is to make the faith of our acceptance depend upon our emotions or feelings, as we saw above; whereas 'the word' is the only true basis of faith; on compliance with which all the promises become ours. We forget the Saviour endured this, and yet was just as acceptable to the Father as when His emotion were the opposite. And now, as we are called to 'endure hardness,' and it is given us 'to suffer with

Christ,' and also to bear some 'afflictions for a moment,' we must certainly not consider any *one state of feeling* the *only acceptable one*. For if, 'when need be,' we are in heaviness, then heaviness must be *felt*. If to endure hardness, then hardness must be *felt*. And if we are to have 'afflictions' then we must sometimes *feel* 'afflicted.' You therefore see that if you take one class of emotions to be the evidence of your acceptance, when you feel thus, your faith in God will abound. But, since our feelings necessarily change and vary, as we have seen above, our faith in this case will sometimes be lost, and we fall into consequent weakness and sadness, if not into gloom and discouragement. Nay, such anchor-ground is too unstable. We need the immovable promise of God, which holds both 'sure and steadfast,' amid all the varying storms, winds, and rolling billows that come upon us.

"The only true test point required of us is in the will. If this be true,—if it be in the heart to say, 'Thy will be done,' we are accepted, let our feelings be what they may; 'for where there is a willing mind, it is accepted.' Ah, this living by feeling, instead of by faith, has made sad havoc of many a promising disciple. It reverses the order of God, and keeps the soul off its only true foundation—the promise of the Father. It is being much as the spoiled child, who, because it is not permitted constantly to feed upon sweetmeats, but is called by its parent to partake of substantial fare, and sometime to take that which is bitter, and also to go forth and endure that which is 'hard and afflicting' loses confidence in the love and wisdom of its father, and sadly refuses to do his will.

"Oh! my brother, let your motto be,—'Not my will but thine be done.' 'Do unto me as seemeth unto thee good,' and all will be well.

"Remember, 'He sitteth as a refiner and purifier of silver, whose business it is, not to see there is no fire to try us, and no dross revealed, but to see that the fire gets not too hot, lest it injure and destroy; nor too cool, lest it do not accomplish its end, the purification of the heart from all its selfish nature.

"Neither is He at a loss for fuel from which to make these purging fires. They come from any and every circumstance around us, that is needful to cross our wills; from many little things connected with ourselves, our families, our tenderest friends, and the common business of life, and even from our religious services. He will cause a fire to glow forth, giving us a sense of the cross, mortification and death which are necessary to the perfect submission of our wills, and entire acquiescence with God. And if these fiery trials which are to try you, reveal hidden selfishness and sin, as the lance reveals offensive matter not before seen, because lying hid deep within, be not disheartened. It is your physician at work wisely, and accomplishing the object of your desire, a perfect cure. Courage brother! Keep your confidence! The ore must be fused before the dross can separate and pass off. We must die in order to live. And His soothing encouragement to you is, 'And after you have suffered awhile, I will strengthen, establish and perfect you.'"

"Now unto Him that is able to do exceeding abundantly above all that we ask or think, according to the power that worketh in us, unto Him be glory in the church by Christ Jesus throughout all ages, world without end. Amen."

INDEX OF TEXTS.

	PAGE.			PAGE.			PAGE.
Gen. 5, 21, 22,	9	Ps. 48, 15,		7	Isaiah 35, 10,		91
" 3, 2,	28	" 51, 10-13,		7	" 40, 1,		142
" 6, 12,	99	" 60, 6,		13	" 1, 4,		164
" 5, 22,	99	" 29, 2,		13	" 10, 20,		164
" 4, 24,	100	" 145, 17,		21	Jer. 4, 14,		30
" 6, 5,	101	" 101, 5,		35	" 48, 10.		192
" 6, 9,	103	" 97, 10,		59	Ezek. 36, 25-27		9
" 6, 11,	184	" 119, 104,		60	" 14, 14,		106
" 17, 1,	208	" 119, 113,		60	Micah 6, 8,		175
Ex. 15, 11,	20	" 139, 122,		60	Zech. 12, 8,		105
" 20, 3,	26	" 119, 63,	60,	70	Mal. 3, 7,		137
" 19, 52,	124	" 45, 7,		63	Matt. 16, 25,		10
Lev. 20, 7,	124	" 119, 97,		75	" 11, 19,		15
" 11, 44	10, 123	" 119, 11, 14, 15,		75	" 10, 25,		15
" 19, 15,	72	" 34, 1,		79	" 11, 5,	39,	70
Joshua 24, 15,	121	" 125, 1,		84	" 1, 21,	40,	229
I Sam. 2, 2,	21	" 37, 4,		94	" 19, 19		41
II Sam. 6, 14-16,	91	" 97, 12,		94	" 5, 43-48		55
I Kings 8, 46,	28	" 33, 1,		94	" 12, 30,		61
" 8, 40,	28	" 149, 2,		95	" 22, 37,	73,	176
" 11, 4,	154	" 119, 14,		95	" 6, 33,		83
Job 1, 1,	9	" 36, 8,		96	" 22, 39,		85
" 1, 8,	14, 31, 105	" 138, 6,		125	" 5, 44,		89
" 4, 8,	14	" 51, 1, 2,		140	" 5, 12,		94
" 8, 13,	14	" 145, 10-12		145	" 5, 48,	104,	207
" 11, 3,	14	" 16, 10,		164	" 11, 11,		105
" 34, 7, 8,	14	" 15, 3,		231	" 25, 29,		144
" 9, 15, 20,	30	Prov. 20, 9,		29	" 7, 20,		171
" 14, 4,	31	" 8, 13		59	" 10, 34,		180
" 22, 11-15,	108	Eccl. 7, 20,		29	" 44, 45,		206
" 1, 5,	109	Isaiah 6, 3,		21	" 5, 48,		213
" 29, 7-17,	110	" 1, 16,		26	" 23, 15,		226
" 2, 9,	110	" 6, 5,		31	Mark 7, 21-24,		34
" 1, 21,	222	" 64, 6,		31	" 16, 15,		85
Ps. 24, 3, 4,	6	" 62, 1		65	Luke 14, 33,		69

INDEX OF TEXTS.

	PAGE.
Luke 22, 39,	85
" 10, 30,	85
" 4, 34,	164
" 1, 74, 75,	229, 165
" 1, 73–75,	184
" 1, 6,	184
John 17, 17,	9, 143, 171, 182
" 5, 44,	11, 70
" 14, 21,	78, 92
" 4, 24,	79
" 15, 19,	88
" 16, 22,	92
Acts 2, 4, 41,	8
" 15, 9,	10, 211
" 26, 18,	10, 211
" 2, 44, 45,	43
" 2, 28,	92
" 13, 52,	93
" 5, 32,	195
Rom. 8, 12, 13,	4
" 12, 1,	10, 125
" 7, 14,	32
" 14, 7,	44
" 8, 14,	50, 76
" 12, 11,	83
" 12, 20,	89
" 14, 17,	92
" 10, 10,	140, 143
" 9, 30,	211
" 5, 1,	211
" 5, 5,	214
" 13, 10,	215
" 14, 18,	233
Cor. 3, 1,	4
" 4, 20,	8
" 2, 12,	12
" 10, 6,	48
" 10, 31,	48
" 1, 26–28,	71
" 13, 1,	91
" 7, 1,	124
" 9, 27,	135
" 6, 11,	138
" 13, 4,	156

	PAGE.
I Cor. 1, 2,	201
" 5, 11,	202
" 3, 1, 3,	203
II Cor. 7, 1,	4
" 6, 18,	80
" 6, 10,	90
" 13, 8,	174
Gal. 5, 19–21,	4
" 5, 22, 23,	41
" 6, 2,	44
" 5, 22,	93, 95
" 3, 24,	211
" 2, 20,	219
Eph. 4, 24,	21, 159, 164, 184
" 6, 6,	67
" 4, 11–13,	104
" 4, 22,	219
" 4, 29,	231
" 6, 5–8	232
Phil. 2, 3, 3,	44
" 4, 12,	46
" 3, 1,	95
" 4, 4,	95
" 3, 18, 19,	190
" 3, 12,	211
" 3, 12–15,	213
Col. 3, 2,	44
" 3, 8,	56
" 1, 28,	208
I Thess. 3, 13,	2
" 5, 23,	3, 5, 9, 53, 189, 202
" 1, 7,	5
" 5, 24,	51
" 5, 16,	95
" 3, 12, 13,	129
" 5, 23, 24,	176
I Timothy 6, 12,	180
II Tim. 3, 12,	17, 72
" 3, 16, 17,	104, 208
" 2, 11, 12,	223
Titus, 3, 5, 6,	203
Heb. 6, 1,	5
" 12, 14,	6, 13

	PAGE.
Heb. 13, 14,	162, 178, 229
" 11, 10,	41
" 11, 26,	41
" 13, 16,	44
" 9, 9,	63
" 11, 25,	72
" 10, 25,	86
" 10, 32–34	87, 168
" 11, 4,	98
" 5, 9,	140
" 2, 10,	211
" 12, 15,	224
James 4, 8,	30
" 5, 19, 20,	136
" 4, 4,	171
I Peter 1, 16,	2
" 1, 8,	7, 93, 96
" 1, 15,	8
" 5, 5,	35
" 1, 5,	130, 139
II Peter 2, 8,	64
" 1, 10, 11,	129
" 1, 5–7	182
" 1, 4,	203, 230
I John 3, 9,	2, 34, 191, 202
" 1, 9,	10, 33, 48, 126, 237
" 1, 8,	32
" 1, 7,	34, 120
" 5, 3,	74, 226
" 4, 1,	77
" 4, 20,	86, 214
" 3, 14,	86
" 3, 17,	86
" 3, 8,	138, 190
" 2, 15,	171
" 4, 12,	216
Jude 14–15,	100
" 24,	131
Rev. 4, 8,	13
" 22, 17,	60
" 3, 16,	37
" 12, 11,	136
" 21, 27,	229

www.ingramcontent.com/pod-product-compliance
Lightning Source LLC
Chambersburg PA
CBHW022354040426
42450CB00005B/180